Sisterhood as Power

Sisterhood as Power

The Past and Passion
of Ecclesial Women

Mary Ann Donovan, S.C.

CROSSROAD · NEW YORK

1989

The Crossroad Publishing Company
370 Lexington Avenue, New York, N.Y. 10017

Printed in the United States of America

Library of Congress Cataloging-in-Publication Data

Donovan, Mary Ann.
   Sisterhood as power : the past and passion of ecclesial women /
Mary Ann Donovan.
      p.   cm.
   Includes index.
   ISBN 0-8245-0961-7
   1. Nuns.   2. Monastic and religious life of women.   I. Title.
BX4200.D66   1989
255'.9—dc20   89-35833
                                                            CIP

For Mary Lou, Sue, and Elizabeth

Contents

Introduction

The sisterhood of ecclesial women is rooted in baptism, the sacrament of initiation common to all Christians. Women and men share in it equally, affirming in it a common faith and being affirmed by it in a common discipleship. The meaning of that common faith has been debated for millennia and those debates are the stuff of the history of doctrine. They are not the concern of this book. Rather, this book is concerned specifically with the efforts of women religious to live out their discipleship as ecclesial women.

The ecclesial identity of religious women has been a matter of concern in the United States since 1983. Identity is shaped in a situation as well as by efforts to resolve the questions "Who am I?" and "Who do you say I am?" In the first chapter I review the situations in which religious life has developed, attending to how religious (and religious women in particular) have expressed their ecclesial identity and to how the church has viewed that identity.

A related issue is that of ministry. Ministry is one way in which discipleship expresses itself. The issues of the development of the ecclesial identity of women religious and the development of women's role in ministry in the church are tightly interwoven. There are significant issues involved in the relationship between the service of witness and the service of public leadership. In chapter 2 I survey the development of women's roles in ministry.

Women religious have played a significant role in the local church in the United States. In turn, the unfolding history of the country has been a factor both in the development of women's religious life and in the forms of ecclesial ministry in

which women engaged. In chapter 3 I sketch the outlines of
that history until 1960. During the twenty-five years from
1960 to 1985 the feminist movement affected the sense of
identity of many women in North America. At the same time
the Second Vatican Council and the events surrounding it
effected an upheaval in the Roman Catholic church. These
factors combined to remake the situation of women in the
church, including women religious. One consequence is that
from one point of view "women's issues" came to be seen as a
problem in the church. When I review that twenty-five year
span in chapter 4 I focus on the underlying theological problem that offers a theological answer to the question "What is
woman?"   *1960-85*

These same twenty-five years saw both an alarming exodus
from religious life and a drop in recruitment which has per-
sisted. I propose one possible explanation of this situation in
chapter 5. The new form religious life has taken for many
women religious in these two and one-half decades includes
an understanding of community living, which involves an
appropriate exercise of authority and accountability in the
mutual exercise of leadership. In chapter 6 I examine that
notion and its roots in one of the four great ancient religious
rules, the *Rule of St. Augustine.*

Vatican II has reawakened in religious women an awareness
of their position as "laywomen" vis-à-vis clerics. In that respect in particular the sisterhood of religious women is with
all women of the church. In chapter 7 I explore St. Catherine
of Siena's teaching on the way of life of the ecclesial person and
its particular implications for the service religious women give
to other women. Finally in chapter 8 I reflect on some
qualities that seem particularly valuable for apostolic religious
women in the late twentieth century as such women, in living
out their form of discipleship, come to realize the power of
their sisterhood.

An earlier version of chapter 1 appeared in *Religious Life in
the U.S. Church: The New Dialogue* (New York: Paulist, 1984),
pp. 212–28. Chapter 5 was originally prepared for the Pontifical Commission on Religious Life. It has been rethought

since the preparation of an early version of it appearing in a forthcoming Paulist collection. Parts of chapter 4 were published as "Women's Issues: An Agenda for the Church?" *Horizons* 14 (1987) 283–95 and as "The Bishops on Women: Pursuing Partnership," *Christian Century* 105 (1988) 564–66. Other sections of the book have benefited from presentations to the National Assembly of Vicars of Religious, the Congregation of the Sisters of the Presentation of the Blessed Virgin Mary, the Congregation of the Sisters of Charity of Cincinnati, and a province of the Adrian Dominican Sisters. The advice and support of colleagues and staff at the Jesuit School of Theology at Berkeley, at the Graduate Theological Union, and elsewhere have been invaluable.

1
Ecclesial Identity of Women Religious

What does it mean to be a woman of the church? To claim the title invokes membership, and membership can take differing forms. Every form involves relationship to ecclesial authority. For American apostolic religious that relationship entered a new era when, on Easter Sunday of 1983, John Paul II called on the American bishops "to render special pastoral service to the religious of your dioceses and your country."[1] Without precisely delimiting the nature of the pastoral care to be exercised, the papal letter enumerated several specific recommendations. The introduction of this episcopal responsibility has shifted significantly the way bishops relate to apostolic religious. It will be useful to see how that is so.

Canon 586 of the 1983 Code of Canon Law assures a true autonomy of life to each institute, especially in governance, and also with respect to the spiritual patrimony of the institute. The kind of autonomy in question has to do with the inner life of the group. Of course, not even an institute's inner life takes place apart from the great church since religious are, after all, members of the church, and religious life is a way of life directed toward the living out of baptism. Religious institutes with their proper freedom live and serve within the church. Both the life and service are of concern to the church. The very life of religious is a treasure to the church (as the papal letter again reminds us). The service of religious is directly or indirectly a collaboration in the work of the church. This is certainly of concern to the church. However, in the immediate past bishops have exercised little direct care for

religious. The pope introduces the new note when he directs
bishops to exercise special pastoral care of apostolic religious
so that these religious might "live their ecclesial vocation to
the full."[2] He is reaffirming the bond between religious and
the church. In the reaffirmation John Paul II is entrusting to
his fellow bishops in the United States a certain care for that
bond. In doing so he introduces a change in the way bishops
relate to apostolic religious in this country.

The outcome of the shift is uncertain. On the assumption
that what has happened in the past is significant for the
present, it would be helpful to examine the spectrum of
church teaching on religious life as that teaching mirrors the
changing relationship between ecclesial authority and religious. That story is as long and as complex as the story of the
church itself. What follows is of necessity selective but attends
to the principal developments.[3] These include: first, the situation in the ancient church, with the position taken in the
Council of Chalcedon; second, the situation that developed in
the medieval church, which on the whole is reflected in the
position taken in the Council of Trent; third, the situation that
has been developing in the nineteenth and twentieth centuries and which is reflected in Vatican II. There are three
questions that organize the material within each section.[4]
First, what is the *situation* within which religious life in its
various forms develops in the given period? While religious
life is a gift of the Spirit to the church, the situation in which
that form of life develops is descriptive of the human factors
through which the Spirit works. Second, how do the religious
of a given era typically express their *ecclesial identity?* Third,
in the period how is religious life viewed from the standpoint
of *ecclesial authority?*

THE ANCIENT CHURCH

The situation

The church came into being in the Roman Empire, in many
ways an ordered world in which birth determined one's place

in life. As the church developed, a number of factors contributed to the evolution of religious life in its earliest monastic forms. I will single out four, of which the first is the politics of the Empire. For some Christians the desert was an escape from persecution. Once there, a number of them were inspired to remain, seeking to live a life of holiness. The effort to avoid physical martyrdom resulted for them in the development of an alternate asceticism.[5] At a slightly later date other Christians fled into the desert to escape the morass of mediocrity spreading in the newly Christian cities. Fervor fueled development of an austere alternate lifestyle.

A second factor that led Christians to seek to live the gospel in this way was the influence of the work of Origen. This Alexandrian teacher offers an optimistic assessment of the powers of human nature to attain sanctity. He stresses the inalienable freedom of human nature as one of the two forces driving fallen humans back to God, providence being the other. That freedom can and must be used to acquire virtue which is won only by discipline. He uses the great metaphors of the journey, of growth, and of struggle to discuss the Christian's return to God. His work inspired generations of ascetics.[6]

A third factor that must be considered is socioeconomic. Until recently many scholars found a socioeconomic impetus toward life in the desert in the social crisis occurring in the Egyptian villages from which the first monks were drawn. In this view the typical peasant of the time was abrasively independent, seeking to govern his own life in as total as possible a disengagement from the restraints of his neighbors. But complete detachment was out of the question. Economic insecurity, taxation (leveled on the village as a whole rather than on the individual), and the need to cooperate in controlling the water of the Nile "forced households of natural egoists into constant, humiliating, and friction-laden contact and collaboration with their fellows."[7] Flight was the instinctive reaction of the farmers, and flight into the desert with escape from insurmountable economic burdens was a route offered by the nascent monastic movement. Current scholarship challenges this view.[8]

Finally, as we move through and beyond the founding
period of the third and fourth centuries, a fourth factor comes
into play: the great migrations of peoples from Asia into Europe. Under the impact of this massive relocation the totter-
ing Roman Empire finally collapsed. The subsequent story of
monasticism in the West is deeply involved with the recivilization of Europe.

Ecclesial identity

Such is the situation in which religious life developed under
the impetus of the Spirit in the ancient church. How did the
religious of that era typically express their ecclesial identity?
The earliest among them understood themselves as laypeople
who lived the life of hermits like the great Antony.[9] Very early,
partially under the impact of the need for mutual direction
and edification, communal forms of the life developed. For
Pachomius, a fourth-century founder of cenobitic monastic life
in Egypt, a key element in the ecclesial identity of the monk
was obedience.[10] The monk, like the nun in the monasteries
directed by Mary, Pachomius's sister, was to attempt to live a
life perfect in morals, with manual work and regular fasting.
Obedience to the abbot within the framework of community
life was central.

Basil and his sister Macrina, who lived in Cappadocia a
generation or two after Pachomius, transformed the ecclesial
identity of the monk and nun.[11] Monasticism was conceived
as a kind of communal living organized around the intent to
help members live together in charity. Certain members were
to assume responsibility for the spiritual direction of the
monks; there is no indication that these directors were priests.
While solitude had its role as the place where a new spiritual
tranquillity would be won, members were to experience the
new form of community life through mutual spiritual as-
sistance. There is no question that the superior was in charge
of the community, and the members were expected to accept
the superior's regulations. In fact obedience was the principal
ascetic practice.

Benedict of Nursia was the great Western monastic founder

of the early sixth century, whose sister Scholastica collaborated with him.[12] While Benedict drew on Pachomius and Basil (among others), his basic insight was a bit different. He saw the essence of monastic life as a school for the Lord's service. The fundamental attitude is to listen for the Master with the heart. To this end the relationship between abbess or abbot and nun or monk becomes one of spiritual parenting implying the duty of spiritual guidance. Yet the group assembled in chapter retains an important role in governance.

For Benedict and Scholastica, Basil and Macrina, Pachomius and Mary the monk or nun was a layperson living a particular form of Christian life within the church. The identity of the member of the community might be expressed in terms of communal living under obedience to an abbot, common life in charity, or the school for the service of the Lord. The well-regulated monastery was an ordered society. Just as in late Roman society every person had a place and moved within it, so too was it the case in the monastery. Humanly speaking, this very stability was part of the appeal when the social order collapsed.

Attitude of ecclesial authority

Many individual bishops lived a form of monastic life, and some were also revered as founders. Among the latter were Basil and also Augustine. Gregory the Great, Bishop of Rome in the late sixth century, was intimately connected with the monastic movement. Prior to his election Gregory was already himself a monk and the founder of monasteries. He is the first of a long line of men who came to the papacy from the religious state.[13] Before and after coming to ecclesiastical office he acted and wrote in favor of monastic life. His work helped to shape religious life in the Middle Ages. However, the weight attached to his writing on monastic life is primarily that which derives from his holiness of life in combination with his wisdom.

The canons of the Council of Chalcedon in 451 offer the clearest example of ecclesial authority acting as such toward religious life on a broad scale. The canons betray both a sense of the relationship of religious to the church and a sense of the authority embodied in the council with respect to that life. The canons are disciplinary. Canon 4 indicates both what was expected of monks and what was deplored among them.[14] Things expected include that they were to be subject to the bishop, to embrace quiet, to attend only to fasting and prayer, and to remain in the places in which they renounced secular life. As to what was deplored, monks were not to busy themselves in ecclesiastical or secular affairs, nor take part in them, leaving their own monasteries, unless permitted to do so for any necessary purpose by the bishop of the city. Canons 7 and 8 forbid the assumption of secular function or military service and place monks who are clerics explicitly under the bishop's jurisdiction. Canon 16 forbids monks and consecrated virgins to marry.

These canons respond to specific difficulties. The history of the period abounds in lawless monks, wandering from place to place.[15] Just before the council for a number of years monks of disputing parties had roiled the ecclesiastical waters from Alexandria to Constantinople. The council knows itself as authority in the church with power to regulate the lives of church members, and so it acts to correct the disturbance. The relationship to the local bishop is seen to be critical and is carefully safeguarded. This relationship will remain central, although with differing nuances, as the story unfolds.

THE MEDIEVAL CHURCH

This second section is concerned with the almost one thousand years between the pontificates of St. Gregory the Great (590–604) and St. Pius V (1566–72). In that timespan, three major developments occurred within religious life with significant consequences for religious life today. These were the transformation of monasticism and the emergence of two new forms of religious life, the mendicant orders in the thirteenth century and the clerks regular in the sixteenth century.[16]

Transformation of monasticism

Factors transforming monasticism include exemption, new roles for monks, and the emergence of religious orders organized as separate houses owing allegiance to a common motherhouse. An understanding of the practice of exemption is basic to an understanding of the relationship between religious and ecclesial authority in this period. Exemption concerns removal from the authority of the local bishops. On the one hand, wealthy lay patrons increasingly retained influence and privileges in the monasteries. Where this happened, monasteries tended to transfer external allegiance from the bishop to the patron. On the other hand, as time passed the pope granted exemption to more and more monasteries, acting sometimes as temporal and sometimes as spiritual lord. This situation applies both to monasteries of men and of women.[17] A further complication affected the men. As larger numbers of monks were ordained, exemption removed men who were exercising priestly functions in the dioceses from the control of the local bishop. Money was involved in terms of profits from the lands, military levies on the dependents of the monasteries, and various benefices. As the relative strength of bishops, pope, abbots, and abbesses varied, it was inevitable that conflicts would occur.

In addition to exemption, another factor changing monastic life was the broadening of the monks' participation in missionary activity and in education. Celtic monks like Columbanus were pioneers in the European mission field. It was through mission work that the monks took the first step toward the recivilization of Europe. The second step came through the development of the monastic school. Since recruits often were not literate and literacy came to be required (at least of choir monks), schools were begun. Together with the episcopal schools of the early medieval period, the monastic school is the germ of the medieval university. More immediately, the monastic schools served as training grounds for bishops. The abbess Hilda provided such fine preparation that five bishops were drawn from her monastery at Whitby.[18]

A third factor transforming monasticism was the emergence of religious orders or congregations organized as groups of houses following one rule and dependent on one motherhouse. Cluny, founded in 910, was the first of these; it followed the practice of making other houses dependent on Cluny from the time of its fourth abbot, Odilio (994–1049), and reached its zenith under his successor Hugh (1049–1109).[19]

Situation

The situation that witnessed this transformation of monasticism was the world of feudal Europe. The dominant rule was Benedictine, so the monastery continued to be seen as the school of the Lord's service. Religious continued to express their ecclesial identity as disciples of Christ, living in a monastery in obedience to the abbot or abbess, with the obligation to recite the office in choir. In terms of the social order, monk related to abbot somewhat as vassal to lord. The abbot, in turn, had various relationships of lordship or vassalage to other abbots, bishops, lords, and the pope.

Attitude of ecclesial authority

From the viewpoint of ecclesial authority, it was Pope Gregory VII (1073–85) who had the most significant effect. Himself a monk, he set out to reform the church on the pattern of a monastic order. Exemption, applied now to entire congregations, was used to strengthen the supreme power of the papacy. After Gregory's time exemption was increasingly extended and often abused. The pope tended to see it as a right to intervene freely in exempt monasteries. Religious tended to view exemption as total independence not only from the local bishop but also from the pope himself.[20]

Shift in situation

Meanwhile, although the economy was still land-based, towns (many of which first grew up around the monasteries) were flourishing. The late twelfth and early thirteenth centuries saw a burgeoning of wealth. It was the time of the Crusades, of penitential journeys for the building of churches in northern France, of the communal movement everywhere: in the Midi and in Northern Italy, on the Rhine and in Flanders. With the coming of the Cathari it was also the time of the rise of heresy as a mass movement. In this situation the mendicant orders appeared and swept across Europe.

Ecclesial identity of mendicants

The mendicants were geared to preach the gospel while living radical gospel poverty.[21] It is true their rules owed much to monasticism. The friars continued to live in common under a superior and to recite the office in choir. However, in contrast to medieval monastic practice, houses as well as individual members depended on alms, members moved from house to house as required, and they engaged in preaching for which they prepared by intense study. Poverty and preaching were key. Granted this internal identity, the founders related themselves to the work of the universal church through the pope. By the thirteenth century the papacy enjoyed true supremacy. The Dominicans, in particular, made a point of strict obedience to pope and bishop to facilitate the work of preaching and to assure the support of local bishops. Francis of Assisi sought a similar relationship but approached it differently. He requested a cardinal protector for his order, who was to represent the order at the curia and to the hierarchy, in order to smooth its path in the church and to keep from the order any shadow of heresy. It should be noted that the potential for conflict was quite real where pope, bishop, and religious superior all had claims on obedience.

Attitude of ecclesial authority

After initial approval, the great struggles with ecclesial authority developed from the exemption of the mendicants and also around the question of Franciscan poverty. An issue of equally great significance but fought less fiercely at the time

was the role of women in the new orders. The exemption
struggle was a fight in which bishops, vicars, and secular
clergy on the university faculties engaged the mendicants.
While lasting a century, ultimately it was resolved in favor of
the mendicants who consistently had favored the doctrine of
papal primacy. Franciscan poverty raised embarrassing questions since the friars insisted that the renunciation of property
"singly and in common" was an essential element in the way
of life Christ himself had taught his apostles.[22] This was a
radical reinterpretation of the scriptures, calling into question
previous exegesis and challenging the way of life of many
church people. A series of thirteenth-century popes addressed questions which had been raised in efforts to interpret the Franciscan rule approved in 1221. The right and
power of popes to respond to this kind of need was accepted.
Meanwhile the friars welcomed papal support against their
enemies.

At this time where were the Marys, the Macrinas, and the
Scholasticas of the mendicant orders? Remember that the
mendicant charism included radical poverty and the preaching of the gospel. The charism corresponded to the need of
the time for witness to poverty and for sound preaching.
While some areas of mendicant houses remained private or
cloistered, the friars were expected to be accessible to those
whom they served. This was not exceptional for male religious.

The situation was different for women. Physical separation
from the world and in particular from the opposite sex is an
ancient ascetic discipline common to males and females. In
the early sixth century Bishop Caesarius of Arles incorporated
that custom into his rule for nuns.[23] The practice was gradu-
ally extended for reasons of physical safety as well as ascetic
discipline. Both Dominic and Francis founded second orders
for women, but ecclesial practice required that these women
be cloistered. Although the stringency of the cloister varied,
in effect the active side of the mendicant charism was excluded.

As for poverty, Clare of Assisi's lifelong struggle to obtain approval of her rule with its practice of radical poverty makes moving reading. It was a struggle she won on her deathbed. There the approved original document was brought to her and "she kissed it many times."[24] She won the fight for radical poverty but her nuns were cloistered. Boniface VIII reinforced this provision for all women religious in 1298. For women, strict cloister joined to solemn vows was the condition of living in the religious state.[25] In sum, ecclesial authority looked with approval on the mendicants, encouraged their poverty, and supported the ministry of the men.

Change in situation

The move from the thirteenth to the sixteenth centuries was not a progression but a decline. It was a period in which religious life and the church to which it belonged mirrored the need for reform. These were the years in which Western Europe suffered the depredations of the Hundred Years' War (conventionally dated 1337–1453). In four of these same years (1347–51) the Black Death decimated Europe. In the fourteenth and fifteenth centuries the abuse of exemption escalated to scandalous proportions. Superiors could hardly initiate reform within congregations as religious could easily remove themselves from obedience to their own superiors; the papal curia readily granted such exemptions. This is the dark side of the close interrelationship between the church and religious life. At the time reform of religious life demanded reform of pope and curia, but pope and curia lived as princes, in a style rivaling that of the rulers of the newly emerging nation states. The time was increasingly ripe for Luther's call to reform, a call that would echo across Europe in the early sixteenth century. In this situation, in the same early decades of the sixteenth century that saw the start of Luther's work, there arose another new form of religious life, the apostolic form represented by the clerks regular.

Ecclesial identity of clerks regular

Clerks regular were ordained male religious who lived by a rule and took as their principal task the exercise of apostolic

zeal, especially through the practice of the spiritual and cor-
poral works of mercy. The Jesuits are representative of this
group. Bangert indicates that Ignatius of Loyola

> set aside four ancient and key forms of the monastic structure:
> lifelong residence in one community; decision-making on ma-
> jor issues by individual communities assembled in chapter;
> the choosing of its superior by each individual community; the
> chanting of the divine office in choir. Ignatius . . . elected that
> detachment, mobility, disposability be the Jesuit marks.[26]

As a key concept Ignatius further insisted that the superior be
in every way the spiritual father of the individual subject. In
this respect Ignatius incorporated a practice of ancient monasticism. As to the founder's expression of the ecclesial identity
of the Society of Jesus, John O'Malley states that the papacy
and the Society were joined in Ignatius's mind

> in the scope of their directly pastoral concerns. The approval of
> the Society and of the *Spiritual Exercises* by the papacy facili-
> tated the apostolic effectiveness of the Society, and especially
> made it capable of transcending diocesan and national bound-
> aries. The pope, as 'universal pastor', symbolized and helped
> implement the worldwide vision that animated the Jesuits'
> concept of their 'missions'.[27]

The Society of Jesus was approved by Pope Paul III in 1540.
Ecclesial authority at this time approved of the new form of
religious life represented by the Jesuits. Other forms of religious life remained in need of reform.

Attitude of ecclesial authority

By the mid-sixteenth century ecclesial authority moved
decisively toward reforming religious life. Among the decrees
of its twenty-fifth session, the Council of Trent promulgated a
decree on religious and one on general reform. As noted
above, in the fourteenth and fifteenth centuries it was difficult
to reform religious life when cardinals and prelates lived scan-
dalously. The two levels of reform were paired in the Triden-

tine decrees. The first chapter of the decree on general reform dealt with cardinals and prelates, requiring them to live a simple and frugal life. They were forbidden to use the goods of the church to increase the fortune of their parents and friends.[28] The decree dealing with religious was not a systematic treatise on religious life; rather, it was a systematic correction of abuses.[29] Basically, religious were asked to live according to the rule they accepted when received into the congregation. Other points of concern were poverty, life outside the religious house, and vows. Nuns were bound by cloister.

In implementing these decrees Pius V obliged all women who were living in community in simple vows without cloister to make solemn profession and accept strict cloister.[30] Here he exceeded the requirements of Trent. Despite the efforts of Boniface VIII, groups like the Sisters of Penance, attached to the Dominican order, had continued to live in common with the three simple vows and no strict obligation of cloister. Julius II had explicitly permitted this.[31] Following the directive of Pius V, many groups of Ursulines who had been founded as apostolic institutes accepted cloister. In the future religious life could accommodate neither Francis de Sales and Jane de Chantal's original vision for the Visitandines, nor Mary Ward's movement, nor the Daughters of Charity of Louise de Marillac and Vincent de Paul. The Visitandines were cloistered. Mary Ward's group was suppressed for almost a century. The Daughters of Charity simply did not become religious; they were constituted as a pious association with private vows. In a memorable conference Vincent de Paul told the sisters to remember "that they are not in a religious order, as this state is unsuitable to the duties of their vocation."[32]

THE NINETEENTH AND TWENTIETH CENTURIES

The Situation

Vincent spoke to the sisters not long after the Peace of Westphalia in 1648 brought to a close the fratricidal wars of religion. One of his great French contemporaries was René Descartes (1596–1650), who turned philosophy toward preoccupation with the thinking subject rather than with the objects of thought. Later, Thomas Hobbes (1588–1679) and John Locke (1632–1704), English philosophers exposed to Cartesian thought, laid the foundations of naturalism (Hobbes) and of liberalism (Locke). The rationalism of their day gave way to the Age of Enlightenment in both France and England. The Enlightenment in turn drew to a close with the revolutions of the late eighteenth century. By the opening of the nineteenth century the worlds of philosophy, of science, and of politics had all been turned upside down. The maps of Europe and of the New World had been redrawn. The winds of democracy were blowing through the social order, and religious life in Western Europe again lay in ruins. One study maintains:

> On the eve of the French Revolution, worldwide membership in all the men's religious orders stood at approximately 300,000; by the time the Revolution and the secularizations which followed had run their course in France and the rest of Europe, fewer than 70,000 remained. [33]

The Jesuits had been suppressed by the church at the instigation of the Bourbons. Some orders had been suppressed by the state; others died by attrition. The following description of the situation sounds in some respects contemporaneous: "The few scattered religious who remained were old and shell-shocked. Some prophets of doom predicted the demise of religious life as a whole." But note how the passage closes: "In fact, the way had been cleared for a revival and recovery of religious life." [34]

Ecclesial identity of religious

In the nineteenth-century situation numerous congregations dedicated to apostolic life, especially teaching, were founded. Old orders like the Dominicans and the restored Jesuits dedicated the energy of vast numbers of their members to that apostolate. Education, a critical need of the

time, was made more urgent by the combination of immigration (on a scale not seen in the previous fifteen hundred years)
with the rise of democracies. In these circumstances many if
not most religious found their apostolic identity as educators.
Here one meets women like Elizabeth Ann Seton and men
like John Bosco. The ecclesial identity of such religious was
shaped in a church which from 1848 was increasingly closed to
the liberal movement of the times and increasingly centralized on the papacy.

Attitude of ecclesial authority

The first harbingers of change could be detected, nonetheless, in the church's outlook on religious life. Three stand out.
First, Pius IX was concerned with the quality of candidates for
religious life. In a ten-year process dedicated to preparation of
a document on religious life, it became apparent that one
problem was the practice of admitting sixteen-year-old candidates directly to solemn vows. The change suggested by the
papacy was to oblige all orders and congregations to permit a
three-year period of simple perpetual vows before solemn
profession. Superiors general were opposed because they
feared the loss of vocations and economic damage from the
delay of priestly ordinations. The pope convened the superiors general in Rome in 1854 to point out that economic
interest simply must cede to the internal reform of the orders.
He himself wrote an introduction to the decree enforcing the
new arrangement[35] in which he urged religious to insert
themselves more in the pastoral ministry through association
with the secular clergy. Are there not here foreshadowings
both of today's concern for quality over quantity of candidates
for religious life, and of the late twentieth-century thrust
toward closer collaboration in the apostolate?

This first point evidently concerns male religious. The second point concerns the women. So many women's congregations were founded in the nineteenth century that this
was one of the factors that led Leo XIII to clarify the status of
religious with simple vows. In 1900 he recognized them as

true religious.[36] Following his lead and that of the Norms of
1902, Canon 488 of the 1917 Code identified such congregations of either sex as religious. Their status remains
unchanged by present church law.

A third point serving as an indicator of change appears in
the early twentieth century. It concerned the education of
religious, especially sisters. Sisters in the United States began
full-scale attendance at institutions of higher learning in 1918
in response to state and regional certification requirements for
teachers and hospital accrediting agencies' requirements for
registered nurses. In 1941 Sister Bertrande Meyers, DC, in
her doctoral dissertation, "The Education of Sisters," at-
tempted to evaluate the effects on women religious of this
large-scale attendance at Catholic and secular colleges and
universities. The dissertation revealed widespread dissatisfac-
tion of major superiors with the education of their sisters. In
1950 the Holy See called an international congress of religious
men and women to discuss major problems, including the
education of sisters. From such beginnings came the Sister
Formation movement in this country and the establishment of
Regina Mundi as an international center for the education of
sisters in Rome. Such efforts provided preparation for the
women religious who assumed leadership in the years following Vatican II.

From a broader perspective the 110 years between 1848
and 1958 were marked by the church's hostility to most of
what the modern world has to offer. Pius IX condemned the
proposition: "The pope can and must try to achieve a reconciliation and a settlement with progress, liberalism, and modern civilization."[37] Leo XIII condemned Americanism, and
Pius X modernism. During the same years increasingly so-
phisticated historical studies contributed to the liturgical and
biblical renaissance. The definitive loss of papal temporal
power, two World Wars, and the unleashing of the atom in
effect created a different world. By the mid-twentieth century
the time was once more ripe for renewal. It is not surprising
that a crowning achievement of John XXIII's Council is *Gaudium et Spes*.

Vatican II's teaching on religious life marks the conclusion of these two centuries and the turning toward an as yet open future. The principal documents are well known: *Lumen Gentium* and *Perfectae Caritatis*, together with Paul VI's *Ecclesiae Sanctae*, which gives the norms for implementation of the renewal required by the two conciliar documents. Also included here is Paul VI's exhortation to renewal, *Evangelica Testificatio*.[38] Vatican II's treatment of religious is in keeping with the council's pastoral character. In *Lumen Gentium* it described the relation of religious to the church.[39] In *Perfectae Caritatis* it called religious to the work of renewal.[40] That work has been the task of the years since the council. Religious men and women have struggled mightily to respond to the call of the church that they might be more nearly and more clearly signs of Christ in this troubled world.

CONCLUSION

From so sweeping a survey it is perhaps more true to say that we may draw suggestions for reflection than that we may draw a conclusion. First, as to the *situation* in which religious life develops: historically, the three major forms of religious life have been monastic, mendicant, and apostolic. It would be useful to reflect on the parallel between the situation, the spirit, the ethos of an age and the form of religious life that developed in that age. Characteristic of the situation of both the late Roman Empire and the early monastic movement was an ordered society. Feudal-style relationships prevailed both in medieval society and in the transformed monasteries. There was a correspondence between the life and work of the friars and the mass movements of the late twelfth and early thirteenth centuries. Later, as the emerging nation states sent out their generals and explorers, so the church sent out its societies of apostles and missionaries. If this be true, it is also true that the world has changed radically these last two hundred years. What is the new form that will correspond to the

new age? Some suggest that it may be found among the
Missionaries of Charity. However, admirable as are Mother
Teresa, her sisters, and their work, this group of missionaries
represents the adaptation of post-Tridentine apostolic life to a
twentieth-century need and not a truly new form of religious
life. In fact the flourishing situation of traditional forms of
religious life in the Third World countries confirms the correspondence between the situation in those countries and the
First World situation that originally gave rise, for example, to
the women's apostolic congregations of the nineteenth century. While it is apparent that earlier forms of religious life
retain validity as they adapt to meet new situations, the
question here is whether under the influence of the Spirit the
church will be blessed with a form of religious life springing
from the situation of the Western church in the late twentieth
century.

This leads to a second area for reflection: a changed sense of
ecclesial identity. Here there are a number of possibilities.
Lozano has remarked that studies of the new constitutions of
women religious reveal a feminist spirituality,[41] a spirituality
which in many cases has been appropriated and reflected in
governmental structures. It is more than simply possible that
a transformation of women's apostolic congregations is under-
way which will rival in significance the transformation of
monastic life in the second half of the medieval period. At the
same time one must consider the significance of the ecumen-
ical community at Taizé, of the hidden apostolates of the Little
Brothers and Sisters of Jesus, of the growth of the secular
institutes, and of the phenomenon of the "noncanonical" communities. All offer material for discernment of where the
Spirit is leading dedicated women and men. Here Gamaliel's
principle is appropriate: if an approach is the work simply of
women and men, it will fail. If it is of God, no one will be able
to overthrow it.

Since religious life is a form of lived discipleship given by
the Spirit for service in, to, and through the church, it is of
concern not only to its members but also to the broader
community of the church and to its bishops. A third area for

reflection concerns *ecclesial authority*. It is a direct implication of the shift in relationship between bishops and religious communities in the United States. A review of history indicates that only in the earlier centuries was relation to the broader church community primarily through the bishop. Through time and the practice of exemption, relationship to the great church was increasingly centered on relationship to the papacy. An effect of the papal intervention is to put American religious in more direct contact with bishops. Widening the dialogue at the diocesan level can lead to an appropriate strengthening of the local churches. Whether this will be fruitful for religious life depends on the type of collaboration that ensues. The way in which American apostolic religious women experience themselves as women of the church has shifted dramatically.

2

Gifts of Women
for Ecclesial Ministry

The issues of the development of the ecclesial identity of
women religious and the development of women's role in
ministry in the church are tightly interwoven. As precursor to
the history of women's roles in church ministry stands the
woman at the well of John 4. Her conversation with Jesus
covered topics ranging from water through her marital status
(or the lack thereof) to the nature of worship. As the conversation unfolds she comes to believe in Jesus as a prophet;
he identifies himself to her as the promised Messiah. John's
story does not end with her conversion. The woman then tells
the people of her city about Jesus. "Many Samaritans from
that city believed in him because of the woman's testimony"
(4:39). Her public witness impels these people to listen to him
for themselves. They ended by being able to say: "This indeed
is the Savior of the world" (4:42). It is in the second part of the
story that discipleship blooms into ministry. The woman's
belief gave rise to witness; her witness brought others to Jesus
and they too recognized him as Savior.

A working definition of ministry is public activity, flowing
from discipleship, leading to the building up of the Christian
community for the sake of the kingdom.[1] It is not a matter of
just any service flowing from discipleship; rather the service
must be public activity. Writing to a community at Rome Paul
lists different public activities, namely, prophecy, service,
teaching, exhortation, and acts of mercy (Rom. 12: 6–8).
These services are clearly performed by a wide and quite
diversified group of people. Romans 16 reflects the scope of

people Paul experienced as engaged in ministry. Paul begins by commending to the Romans Phoebe, the woman who is deacon *(diakonos)* of the church at Cenchreae, asking them to give her whatever help she requires since she has helped many, including Paul (vv. 1–2). He proceeds then to greet Prisca and her husband Aquila, whom he identifies as his fellow workers who have risked their lives for Paul's life. A church meets in their home (vv. 3–4). Among the women he mentions are Mary, "who has worked hard among you" (v. 6), Tryphaena and Tryphosa, "workers in the Lord" (v. 12), and his beloved Persis, another hardworking woman (v. 12). Among other workers at Rome who are greeted by name are Andronicus and Junia. Paul identifies them as his kinsmen and fellow prisoners, and as noteworthy among the apostles (v. 7). Until the thirteenth century the tradition identified the apostle Junia as a woman. Today philological studies affirm the tradition.[2] In one community at Rome Paul knew women and men in a variety of ministerial roles. Furthermore, the story of Phoebe indicates that her ministry was not restricted to Rome. It is reasonable to conclude that the Roman experience reflected the usual practice. What does this contribute to the understanding of the relationship between discipleship and ministry? In the world of the New Testament, active belief in Jesus (which is discipleship)[3] results in ministry, public activity for the building up of the community of believers for the sake of the kingdom. John's story, for example, emphasizes that the woman's encounter with Jesus was the catalyst for fruitful discipleship. To be a Christian is to be called to discipleship. To accept the call to discipleship is to accept the call to ministry.

WOMEN'S MINISTRY IN THE ANCIENT CHURCH

While the notion of ministry itself was quite broad in the New Testament texts, that notion underwent a fairly rapid series of developments by 325 C.E. First, ministry was largely identified with leadership in preaching, teaching, and presiding, and centralized in the bishop. Thomas O'Meara has called this the "episcopalization" of ministry.[4] This development stressed institutional rather than charismatic gifts. By about 110 Ignatius of Antioch presents the bishop as ruling a church, assisted by presbyter and deacon (*Trallians* 2). These three roles became central. In a second development, bishop and presbyter were explicitly recognized as priestly roles. By the beginning of the third century, the ministerial leader was identified as *sacerdos* or *hiereus*, "priest" (Tertullian, *On Chas*. 7.3). An important factor in this development was the influence of the Old Testament. Descriptions of the Israelite priesthood, read ahistorically, were interpreted as prescriptive for Christianity. O'Meara remarks:

> An inspired page no longer struck Christians as a forecast of fulfillment in Christ but as a divine prescription; the Jewish hierarchy of high priest, priest, and levite was admired by Clement of Rome, and then assumed as a theology of ministry a century later by Cyprian of Carthage. Of course, a purely sacerdotal hierarchy was what the first Christians had seen terminated in Jesus Christ.[5]

Ministry, which was becoming understood as leadership centered on the bishop, was also sacerdotalized. The earliest rituals of ordination that we possess are from this time.[6] In a third development, the practice of ordained ministry was focused on a special place. The New Testament records that the church met in a house belonging to Prisca and Aquila, a married couple. This was quite possible while numbers remained small. As the community grew larger, more space was needed.[7] By the third century some houses were set aside for worship. Christian churches were no longer unusual in the year 300, and after persecution ceased in 311 churches became the norm. This shift in place affected at least the style of ministry.

If it is true that the call to discipleship includes a call to ministry, such that discipleship normally finds expression in ministry, then it becomes necessary to reflect upon the ministerial forms available in this situation, as well as to inquire where in this development were the women, those hard-workers whom Paul knew. While ministry was largely sub-sumed under leadership expressed in ruling over the community, teaching it, and presiding over its worship, minis-try was not then (or ever) totally subsumed in this way. In the early period, Gryson points to the easily identifiable minis-terial gifts, including the charismatic gift of prophecy, the work of male and female deacons, and the work of widows and virgins.[8]

The woman prophet was particularly important in the sec-ond century and unfortunately was almost always prominent in unorthodox literature and movements. The apocryphal *Acts of Paul* associates a woman named Thecla with Paul's ministry and introduces her as a prophet. The prophet Helena accom-panies Simon Magus, the prophet Philoumene is with Ap-elles, and Maximilla and Priscilla are the prophet-companions of Montanus. The movements which these women and men led were rejected, as was a prophetic function for women. Tertullian, a Latin writer of the early third century, writes:

> It is not permitted to a woman to speak in church. Neither may she teach, baptize, offer, nor claim for herself any function proper to a man, least of all the sacerdotal office. (*Veil. virg.* 9.1; see also *On bap.* 1, 6.)

This remained true for Tertullian even when he became a Montanist. He then permitted women to prophesy, but no woman might reveal a prophecy during common worship, even though moved by the Spirit. She was required to wait until all had gone out and then report her visions to the heads of the sect (*On the Soul* 9.4). Origen, a Greek contemporary of Tertullian's, takes a similar position. He emphasizes that in Acts 21:9 the daughters of Philip who prophesied did not do it in mixed assemblies. Women in Titus 2:4 teach only younger women. He concludes that women should not guide men.[9]

The ordained ministry of the women deacons underwent quite different developments in different geographic areas as well as in different periods. In Egypt by the early third century, both Clement and Origen recognized that there were women deacons in the church in St. Paul's time. To their knowledge, though, the practice has died out. Origen seems to find Romans 16:1 surprising. He writes: "This text teaches *with the authority of an apostle* that even women are made deacons of the church" (*Com. Rom.* 10:17).

Moving north and east to Syria, one finds clear third-century evidence of women deacons. There is an interesting typology found only here: the bishop is seen as the image of God the Father; the deacon is the image of Christ; the presbyters together image the college of the apostles; the woman deacon is the image of the Holy Spirit.[10] Her functions are to visit, baptize, anoint, and instruct women, and to care for the sick. She does not assist at the Eucharist, as does her male colleague.

By the end of the fourth century the women may serve as messengers (as do their male colleagues), and they also are expected to accompany women in visits to the bishop or deacon. They are ordained members of the clergy, and this continues in the Syrian church to the twelfth century.[11] Gryson indicates that a similar situation is found in the Greek city of Constantinople. Olympias, the friend of Chrysostom, was a deacon. Many others are known by name from the fourth through the sixth centuries. The practice continued in this area to the thirteenth century.

By contrast, the Latin church was, by the end of the fourth century, ignorant of the practice then flourishing in the East. Ambrosiaster (late fourth century) understood Phoebe's role in Romans 16:1 as a "helper." (The Latin New Testament he knew had *ministra* for the Greek *diakonos*.)[12] The only women deacons he knew about were Montanists. The late fourth-century Council of Nimes (394 or 396) had heard rumors that in some place at some time women had been ordained to the diaconate. The council members were not certain what exactly had happened and were ignorant of contemporary Eastern practice. Nevertheless, they condemned the practice. Gryson cites the text:

> It has been reported *(suggestum est)* by certain ones that, contrary to apostolic discipline and unknown until today, women seem to have been, one knows not where, admitted to the Levitical ministry. Since it is improper, the ecclesiastical rule does not permit this innovation. Made contrary to reason, an ordination of this type must be annulled, and care must be taken that no one in the future shows a similar audacity. [13]

The first Council of Orange similarly prohibited such ordinations fifty years later. There the matter rested for the Western church.

Women continued to respond to the call to discipleship, but its expression in public service in the church was limited to the roles of the widows and virgins. Widowhood, a state of life, in the ancient church became associated eventually with certain functions, none of which were liturgical. A very early writer termed widows the "altar of God" (Polycarp, *To Phil.* 4). Altar here had two meanings. First, the widows lived by the generosity of the faithful and so were like altars on which gifts are offered to God. Second, the work of dedicated widows was to fast and offer uninterrupted prayer: thus, they were like altars from which such prayer ascends. Widows recognized as such were "registered" and professed continence. They were to be of mature years; younger women might eventually want to remarry. Virgins resolved to remain continent for the honor of the Lord, vowed continence, and were associated with the widows in ideals and lifestyle. Asceticism and prayer was expected of both groups. When no close relatives were available to support them, virgins, like widows, were supported by the community. A third-century document states:

> When a widow is appointed she is not ordained but she shall be chosen by name . . . But she shall not be ordained because she does not offer the oblation nor has she a liturgical ministry. She is appointed for prayer and this is a function of all Christians. [14]

In summary, in the early church prophecy is a gift associated with unorthodox women. It is recognized only with great

difficulty in orthodox women by the beginning of the third
century. Women deacons emerge in the Syriac church in the
third century and flourish both there and in the Greek church
in the fourth through the sixth centuries, with the practice
continuing into the medieval period. A similar development is
not found in the Latin church. The order of widows and the
group of consecrated virgins emerge early and last throughout
the period of Christian foundations. These women are not
ordained and exercise no liturgical function. Their role is to
pray and fast for the church.

If ministry is a consequence of discipleship and if it is public
activity recognized as such, exercised for the building up of
the Christian community for the sake of the kingdom,
women's ministry during the foundational period of the
church was severely restricted. Only where women deacons
were accepted was a formal role in ministry available. This
formal role associated them publicly with the institutionalized
and ordained ministry of leadership to which were assimilated
the teaching, governing, and sanctifying functions.

This was so not for one reason but for a number of reasons,
including the status of women in late antiquity, the en-
trenched patriarchal system which reinforced the low status of
women, and the prevailing philosophy which further contributed to the prevailing low estimation of women. These three
reasons intersected as ministry developed in a leadership
modality. A public-leadership role like that of the bishop, the
presbyter, or the deacon was not a woman's role in this society.
Furthermore, in a patriarchal society women do not teach
men. Teaching was a critically important role of bishop and of
deacon. In a Platonic world-view, inferiors do not rule superiors. Women, by definition, are inferior to men in this system.
It would therefore be inappropriate for women to exercise any
ministry that gave them positions of superiority over men.
Consequently, women's energies were directed toward the
ascetic way of life. To this extent, it is probably true to say that
the times conspired to truncate women's discipleship.

This picture, while bleak, is not the whole picture. The
development of the ordained ministry sketched here is an

institutional development. It is a given that any movement that endures will be institutionalized. In a sense the institutional church is a necessity of the incarnation. God became a human being, becoming subject to the laws of time and space. God became a historical being. The risen Christ transcends history, but his church continues in history and remains subject to its laws. A historical law connects continuity with institutionalization. The institutional church gives visible form to the society, the community of disciples.

However, Avery Dulles, taking a page from Vatican II (*Lumen Gentium,* especially nos. 6–9), points out that the richness of the reality of the church is best apprehended when people keep in mind that it is not simply an institution.[15] It has at least four other dimensions. First, it is the Body of Christ, the People of God in which every member is vivified by the Spirit who, as life-giver, is also principle of unity. Second, when the grace given by the Spirit comes to expression in the women and men who make up the church, when members live in such a way that grace is manifest in them, then the church is the Sacrament that makes Christ present in the world. Third, the church is Herald, the proclaimer of the coming of Christ. In the words and deeds of its members the church tells the world who Christ is and what his coming means. Fourth, the church is the Servant, present in the world in its members to be of help to all human beings. Those who form the servant-church are called to keep alive hope, to speak the words of comfort to the afflicted and to utter prophecy in the face of injustice.

Those called in this way constitute the church, and the church includes secretaries and waitresses, wives and mothers, and the disaffected as well as those actively working in the institution. The Christian call to discipleship comes to fruition when believers so live that others recognize the presence of Christ. That is the church operating as sacrament, and a life so lived is witness which is a form of ministry. Discipleship comes to fruition when in word or in deed Christians tell the story of Christ, whether these Christians are catechists, writers, parents, teachers, theologians, preachers. The proclama-

tion of the gospel is the church operating as herald, and one
who witnesses in this way is engaging in a form of ministry.
Discipleship comes to fruition when Christians comfort the
mourning, care for the sick, take in the orphaned, give food to
the hungry and drink to the thirsty, protest injustice and fight
oppression, engage in the work of peacemaking in a nuclear-
mad world. This, too, is a form of ministry. Those who minister in these ways are the servant church. The work of the
institutional leader in relation to such forms of ministerial
activity is to encourage, to bring the different activities of
various church members into harmony, to reconcile differences, preserving unity and—while holding opposing
forces in balance—somehow to inspire forward movement.

Note the difference. Witness as form of ministry represents
the fruition of discipleship in the church viewed outside the
institutional dimension. In the first centuries, much attention
was given to leadership in the emerging institution. Leadership and its forms were important issues as the infant
church struggled to shape its identity. In large part because of
the nature of late antique society women were forbidden an
integral role in ordained ministerial leadership. The form of
ministry proper to the church as institution is the role of the
public leader which continues to be barred to women.

DISCIPLESHIP AND MINISTRY IN THE MIDDLE AGES

With the end of widespread persecution in the fourth century, the fall of the Empire in the West in the fifth century,
and the subsequent outreach to the barbarian kingdoms in the
West, a new form evolved for the ministerial expression of
discipleship. Some Christians continued to seek lives marked
by prayer and asceticism like those lived by the order of
widows. The monastic movement institutionalized this form of
life. Eventually other ministerial activities such as care of the
sick and teaching found a place within monasticism. Out-

standing women like the Desert Mothers Mary and Pelagia,[16] Macrina,[17] and Jerome's friend Melania the Elder[18] were numbered among the founders of the movement. Their leadership helped shape earliest monasticism. Increasingly in the time between late antiquity and the high Middle Ages, Christians tended to view monks and nuns as those who "took care of" the religious side of life. Day-to-day living for most people was a matter of survival against high odds: famine, pillage, rape, and war.

Two extraordinary women delineate the beginning and the end of the period. Hilda of Whitby, a seventh-century English abbess, was the foundress of a renowned monastery for women and men. The Venerable Bede narrates her story:

> [She] taught the observance of righteousness, mercy, purity, and other virtues, but especially of peace and charity. After the example of the primitive church, no one there was rich, no one was needy, for everything was held in common, and nothing was considered to be anyone's personal property. So great was her prudence that not only ordinary folk, but kings and princes used to come and ask her advice in their difficulties and take it. Those under her direction were required to make a thorough study of the Scriptures and occupy themselves in good works, to such good effect that many were found fitted for Holy Orders and the service of God's altar. Five men from the monastery later became bishops—Bosa, Aetla, Oftfor, John and Wilfrid—all of them men of outstanding merit and holiness. . . . Christ's servant Abbess Hilda, whom all her acquaintances called Mother because of her wonderful devotion and grace, was not only an example of holy life to members of her own community; for she also brought about the amendment and salvation of many living at a distance, who heard the inspiring story of her industry and goodness.[19]

In Hilda's lifework the church is present as Body of Christ, as Sacrament, as Herald, and as Servant—and the disciple Hilda prepares leaders for the institutional church.

Hildegard of Bingen, who lived in the twelfth century, was also an abbess. Confided to the care of nuns as an oblate at the age of eight (not an unusual practice then), she became abbess by the time she was thirty-six and founded two monasteries. A wise leader, she was also widely known as a visionary, a prophet, and author of works of theology and of music. One of her great concerns was reform of the church.[20]

Hildegard was one of the earliest of a succession of leaders crying out for reform in the centuries before Luther. Shortly after her death, lay movements calling for penance and poverty began to spread in Western Europe. Itinerant preachers proclaimed apostolic poverty and the imitation of Christ on the streets and in the squares, in the houses and in the churches. It is this milieu which in the thirteenth century gave rise to the mendicant orders exemplified by the work of Francis and Dominic discussed in chapter 1. There we saw that by the close of the thirteenth century strict cloister was expected of women entering the religious state.

In the later medieval period other women, laywomen, sought to express discipleship by going out to minister directly to the needs of the poor in the growing cities. Hadewijch and Catherine of Siena offer creative and influential examples of women's efforts to participate actively in ministry in the spirit of the age. Hadewijch, who is becoming better known in English-speaking countries since the translation of her work, is one of the great figures in the Western mystical tradition, an important expounder of love mysticism.[21] She was a laywoman who probably lived in the mid-thirteenth century. She was active in the Beguines, a movement dating from the late twelfth century. These women lived a simple life in common. They came and went, earning their own living (often as weavers or seamstresses), and engaged in care for the sick and in teaching. They made no vows, but they promised chastity while living in the beguinage, and obedience to the statutes, to the mistress of the house, and to church authority. While some groups were dissolved in the condemnation of a heretical group at the end of the thirteenth century, others lasted for many centuries.

Catherine of Siena (1347–80) represents another option. She, too, was a laywoman, a member of the Third Order of St. Dominic. Catherine was the guiding spirit of a group of women and men who were Dominican tertiaries. She gave them spiritual direction, tended the sick and dying of Siena, and worked actively for the reform of the church, most particularly for the return of the papacy from Avignon. Her writings are a rich heritage.[22] Today she is honored as a saint and a doctor of the Roman Catholic Church, with Teresa of Avila one of two women so honored. In her life and teaching she presents an extraordinary model of the ecclesial woman. We will return to her under that guise in chapter 7.

In summary, emergence of the mendicant charism marked the medieval period of the church's history. That charism called for ministering to the needs of the world by apostolic poverty in imitation of Christ, by preaching and teaching. Women members of the second orders of the mendicant foundations were restricted to the cloister. Laywomen like Hadewijch and Catherine gave expression to their discipleship in forms of ministry in keeping with the spirit of the age by participation in lay movements.

BEYOND CONVENT WALLS

The call for reformation climaxed in the sixteenth century. This coincided with the beginnings of the nation states typical of the modern world. With this shift was another one in ministry. From at least the sixth century institutionalized forms of ministry (other than hierarchical leadership) had focused on the monastery. Even the mendicants had retained common life and recitation of the office proper to monastic life, although the males went out from their houses for ministry. In the sixteenth century, religious founders dropped monastic practices like the office in choir, and the pattern of life of the one engaged in ministry was individualized. Angela Merici was one of the first to organize a religious group in this new pattern. She founded the Ursulines in 1535. Following the directive of Pius V, Angela's group eventually was cloistered. Subsequent foundations in the Ursuline tradition divide between the cloistered and "active" groups.

Meanwhile, despite the Roman regulations, groups of women continued to function in active ministry and under vow in various dioceses. To understand continued papal insistence on cloister for nuns it is helpful to remember that Pius V was attempting to correct the abuse of cloister, abuses like those illustrated by the prioress in Chaucer's *Canterbury Tales*. The great Teresa of Avila, a contemporary of Angela's, was equally aware of the problem. To her credit is the reform of the cloistered Carmelite orders of both women and men. Her works, including *The Interior Castle* and *The Way of Perfection*, are among the treasures of Spanish literature and Christian spirituality. Her disciple John of the Cross follows in her tradition.

However, Angela's vision of women actively serving beyond convent walls was not forgotten. Jane Frances de Chantal, in cooperation with Francis de Sales, founded the Visitation Order in 1610. Although she had originally planned an active group, Jane and her sisters were cloistered.[23] The notion that the woman who wanted to minister in a formal way must do so as a cloistered nun was deeply etched in church practice. It took one hundred years for the practice to change, and an additional two hundred years for the practice to receive ecclesiastical approval.

The cloister walls were finally breached by the concerted efforts of Louise de Marillac and Vincent de Paul. They succeeded by duplicity. They explicitly refused to found a religious order. Their intent was to found a group of women to serve the needs of the poor. Vincent writes:

[The Sisters] shall bear in mind that they are not a Religious Order, as this state is unsuitable to the duties of their vocation. Nevertheless, as they are more exposed to the occasions of sin than religious bound to enclosure, having only for Convent the houses of the sick and that in which the Superioress resides, for a cell a hired room, for a chapel their parish church, for a cloister the streets of the city, for enclosure, obedience, with an obligation to go nowhere but to the houses of the sick, or places that are necessary to serve them, for a grille, the fear of God, for a veil, holy modesty, making use of no other form of profession to assure their vocation than the continual confidence they have in Divine Providence and the offering they make to God of all that they are and of their service in the person of the poor, for all these considerations they should have as much or more virtue than if they had made their profession in a Religious Order, and hence they shall strive to comport themselves in all those places with at least as much reserve, recollection and edification as true religious manifest in their convents.[24]

The Daughters of Charity founded by Louise and Vincent succeeded in escaping the cloister by the simple expedient of ministering as laywomen.

Yet foundresses continued to seek approval for non-cloistered women religious. Two hundred years later, in 1831, Catherine McAuley wanted to organize a group of women to minister among the needy. Her congregation, the Sisters of Mercy, requested and, in 1841, received ecclesiastical approval of their constitutions, which called for simple vows and did not require cloister.[25] Following the action of Leo XIII in 1900, the 1917 Code of Canon Law clearly identified as religious the communities of women who make simple vows and are not cloistered.[26] Why did women need this documentation? As laywomen they were quite successfully ministering, making present the church, the community of disciples. What they wanted was formal recognition of their ministry and their ministerial lifestyle. Many of the problems connected with the approval of the constitutions of women's religious orders reflect the continuation of that struggle.

The struggle for the recognition of women who are not cloistered but vowed to service as truly women of the church is part of the struggle of all women. There is more that unites laywomen and sisters than there is dividing them. First, all are women. Second, none of them are part of the ordained leadership of the Roman Catholic church. Third, all share the experience that some of their gifts, their talents, some of the ministries they are able to perform are wanted and accepted in the church and many others are not. All know what it means to have their opinion dismissed in advance simply because it is a woman's opinion. There is a history of women whose opinions did matter, women who made a difference. Those women include Louise de Marillac, Catherine of Siena, and Hadewijch. They include Pelagia and Prisca. Each of them was, and remained, a laywoman. Each worked with clerical leadership, effectively ministering either through or despite the structures of the institution. This number includes Dorothy Day and Jean Donovan. These were laywomen whose expression of discipleship was in ministry to the needs of the world in ways corresponding to their own giftedness. Jean Donovan bore witness even unto death. But she did not die alone. It is important to remember the circumstances of her death. She was one of a group of four women, lay and religious, serving the oppressed in El Salvador.

That is where women belong: together, in the face of oppression. They may face oppression in their own homes or workplaces. The oppressed who call out for their aid may live in North American neighborhoods or in Central American barrios. Like the Samaritan woman, contemporary ecclesial women hear the needs of those they meet in their daily round. They respond by carrying to them the good news of Christ.

Why do so many continue to act as ecclesial women? Perhaps here it is best to answer a question with a question: "Lord, to whom should we go? You have the words of eternal life" (John 6:68). At each stage in the history of Christianity women have developed strategies correlative to their individual gifts. Using these strategies they engage in ministry to build up the church, to build up, restore, reform, repair, energize the community of believers in order that the kingdom of Jesus might come. The role of a woman of the church is the role of a builder of the future. The future that these women work toward is the reign of justice and peace inaugurated when a woman gave birth in a stable to a man who would die on a cross. His resurrection is the pledge that in the end the struggle will not have been in vain.

3
Ecclesial Women in the
U.S. Church, 1780–1960

The situation in which American religious women exercise their role as ecclesial women is that of the local church in the United States. To understand their experience of religious life and the way they have come to express their ecclesial identity it is useful first to think about the country and how it has related to the church. Americans value freedom, independence, and religious tolerance (or, at least, religious pluralism). The Catholic church has a history of intolerance in the name of religious supremacy and claims of its adherents an interior loyalty of mind and will. Regularly that raises the question whether it is possible to be both American and Catholic. The story of American Catholicism can be told as a series of answers to that question, answers whose emphases vary widely from John Carroll and Elizabeth Seton to Dorothy Day and Thomas Merton. But at each step of the story, the situation of religious reflects the experience of American Catholics. So the framework of the story is the framework of American Catholic history. That history falls into three parts: (1) Catholic in the New Nation, 1780–1820; (2) The Immigrant Church, 1820–1920; (3) From Ghetto to Mainstream, 1920–1960. In each part of the story these questions guide reflection: What was the sense of church? Who were the religious and what was expected of them? How were religious accepted? Throughout, this analysis is indebted to the work of three historians of American Catholicism: Jay Dolan,[1] Mary Ewens,[2] and James Hennesey.[3]

CATHOLIC IN THE NEW NATION, 1780–1820

What was the sense of church?

"More than an armed rebellion, the American Revolution was an ideological revolution the effects of which were felt long after the last shot was fired at Yorktown."[4] So Jay Dolan affirms. The real revolution was the shift from a society built on patronage and privilege to one valuing equality and independence. The churches experienced a new spirit of toleration, and Catholics enjoyed the novel experience of full political participation. In this heady atmosphere John Carroll argued that Rome should allow the U.S. church "that Ecclesiastical liberty, which the temper of the age and of our people requires."[5] In the vital step of naming the first bishop, American Catholic clergy saw the need to be *independent* of foreign intervention. Rome granted permission to elect the first bishop (to no one's surprise, Carroll), and he quickly founded Georgetown Academy to educate young men from whom would be drawn future American priests. Carroll's vision was of a country with its own clergy, "men accustomed to our climate, and acquainted with the tempers, manners, and government of the people, to whom they are to dispense the ministry of salvation."[6]

This would lead to an American church. In Carroll's view such a church, while in communion with the See of Rome, would be internally autonomous. To a certain extent, this desire for independence and this hunger for an American church brought about a presbyteral model of the church in the earliest years of the Republic. Finally, Carroll and the majority of American Catholics favored separation of church and state. Thus they endorsed religious pluralism and at the same time were embroiled in a new way of handling church property. It was not until Vatican II that the Catholic church would accept the American tradition of religious freedom. The related question of ownership of property led to a whole series of problems as the church adjusted to its new situation. Meanwhile, Catholics in the new nation experienced their church as independent, American, and taking root in a pluralistic society.

Who were the religious and what was expected of them?

Six congregations of women were established and thrived in the United States during the period 1780–1820,[7] in addition to the Ursulines who were already present in New Orleans when the Louisiana Territory was annexed in 1803. (They had begun their work there in 1727.) Of the new foundations, the Carmelite experience is typical. While the Discalced are strictly contemplative, Carroll wrote to Rome: "Their convent would be a far greater benefit in the future if a school for the training of girls in piety and learning were begun by them."[8] The women refused to take advantage of the dispensation Carroll obtained for them, despite their need for the income a school would bring. In time, Southern women who entered brought sufficient dowry in goods and chattels (including slaves) to enable the community to survive. Adaptation was needed; the bishop wanted it in the works of the community, but this group resisted.

But the canonical norms governing religious life for women continued to present difficulties for American religious women. According to these norms until 1900 a true religious woman made solemn vows and therefore was cloistered.[9] In Europe, where these customs arose, convents were endowed. The primary work of the cloistered woman was to pray the divine office. In this country religious had to support themselves, and most did so by responding to the very real need for teachers. For the great majority the commitment to teaching was in tension with the thrust of a life geared to cloistered contemplation. The ideal constantly held up was the "true religious," that is, the European or cloistered religious. Adaptation was necessary for survival, and the more successful communities modified their practices. In 1829 the Visitandines received Pius VIII's permission to adjust their rules to work in the new environment. Changes enabled them to support themselves by conducting a paying academy, to educate poor girls outside the cloister, to admit day pupils, and to make other adjustments called for by the changes in climate and customs. Other orders, like the Poor Clares whose very nature would have been violated by teaching, did not take root in the new country at this stage.

In founding the Sisters of Charity at Emmitsburg, Maryland, Mother Elizabeth Ann Seton worked with European-trained priests who wanted the rule of the French Daughters of Charity for the sisters. The Daughters had never been bound by solemn vows nor cloistered. Vincent de Paul had been strongly opposed to their becoming religious because, as he said, "Who say 'religious' say cloistered and the Daughters of Charity must go everywhere."[10] His group was a company of women bound by private vows and supported by the wealthy to serve the needs of the poor. Unlike the French sisters, however, the Americans needed to educate paying pupils as well as the poor, since they had to support themselves. So as Carroll remarked, the proposal to join the French community "was soon and wisely abandoned for causes, which arose out of distance, different manners, and habits of the two countries, France and the United States."[11] The work of the Sisters of Charity expanded to meet the need for orphanages and hospitals. In its beginnings the community was an American group using a French rule adapted to the needs of the American church. Eventually, in 1851, the community at Emmitsburg affiliated with the French Daughters of Charity, but daughterhouses in New York and in Cincinnati formed separate congregations, preserving the "American" thrust of the community.

How were religious received?

The reactions to the sisters were largely positive. Sister Rose White wrote to Mother Seton from the orphanage in Philadelphia in 1817: "You have no idea how the lovers of money admire the disinterestedness of those who serve God, and how eagle-eyed they are to all the actions of the sisters. . . ."[12] Carroll wrote in praise of the Carmelites. Protestant and Catholic alike attended the Ursuline schools in New Orleans and in Boston. Negative preconceptions about women religious seem to have been changed by face-to-face meetings.[13]

THE IMMIGRANT CHURCH, 1820–1920

This century-long period is marked by a great influx of immigrants, large numbers of whom were Catholic. During the entire period the sense of church underwent a significant shift, while the roles and the acceptance of religious shifted three times. Characteristic differences mark the ante-bellum church, 1820–60; the Civil War church, 1860–70; and the explosive growth of 1870–1920. Thus it is possible to examine the question concerning church once for the whole period and deal with the religious in the three subperiods.

What was the sense of church?

During this period there was a shift from a presbyterial model to a hierarchical one. The change was first noticeable in Irish communities during the 1820s and 1830s. By the 1850s, most Irish parishes had accepted the hierarchical concept of church. There was resistance to the shift in various ethnic groups, especially Poles, Lithuanians, and Slovaks.[14] However, Dolan remarks that by the 1920s "the clergy controlled the parish, and the tradition of laypeople participating in the organization and government of the local church had come to an end."[15] He outlines a number of reasons for this process, including: (1) by the middle of the nineteenth century, the democratic ideals in religion in America, Catholic and Protestant, had waned, and religion was once more hierarchical in nature with clergy having status and control; (2) the papacy was restored to a central and strong position in the nineteenth century, with—in the diocese and the parish—the bishop and the pastor being seen somewhat as "little popes." In fact, the Third Council of Baltimore in 1884 gives the distinct impression that the bishop *is* the church.[16] The tendency to equate church with organization was well advanced.

Conjoined to the shift from a presbyteral to a hierarchical

model of church was a shift from an Enlightenment piety
(personal and interior) to a baroque piety, resting on a pessi-
mistic view of the human person and emphasizing order,
control, subordination, and disciplinary uniformity.[17] Chinnici has singled out *The Ursuline Manual* of 1844 as an il-
lustration of what happened when a view of the church as the
sole means of salvation joined the hierarchical values of organization and subordination. In this devotional manual we read:

> The authority we are obliged to submit to, is not that of any
> clergyman speaking or acting from himself; but it is the au-
> thority of the entire body of the Pastors of the Church. Each
> clergyman, in the discharge of his functions, acts as the
> Church's deputy. It is in her name, and by her authority, he
> instructs and guides the faithful committed to his care. The
> submission and obedience paid him in this capacity, is paid to
> the Church itself; and in obeying the Church, we obey Jesus
> Christ.[18]

In the view of the writer of the manual, obedience to the
priest is obedience to Jesus Christ. As Chinnici notes, this
position corresponds to what is found in episcopal reflections
and conciliar decrees of the period. The whole rationale pre-
supposes personal weakness, confraternal protection, and hierarchical mediation. The resultant religious sensibility
assured the survival of the church in this country, but it also,
in Chinnici's words, "separated the Church from the world,
facilitated the mystification of authority, and placed order,
external conformity, at the center of the spiritual life."[19] One
might well ask: survival at what price?

THE IMMIGRANT CHURCH: THE ANTE-BELLUM PERIOD, 1820–60

Who were the religious and what was expected of them?

While more communities were present, expectations were
tempered by the pioneering spirit required even in somewhat

more settled areas. Sisters of Providence, fresh from France, were startled when their chaplain proposed to hear their confessions in their backwoods parlor, without entering a confessional or donning a surplice. They were further amazed to meet priests dressed in the flat, lie-down collar and black string tie of the laity, the style common to all American priests before 1884.[20] A hierarchical model of church may have been abroad, but in the early years of the period the spirit of the frontier tempered it.

Numbers of sisters continued to struggle to meet simultaneously the apostolic needs of the U.S. church and the canonical requirements of a cloistered religious life. It may be noted that those who followed rules modeled on Vincent de Paul's adapted more easily. Practices like rising for night office took a toll on the health of teaching sisters. In addition, class-consciousness informed sisters transported from European motherhouses and often pervaded the structures of communities. This affected relations with priests, students, and help, as well as with American postulants. There is a wonderful story told by Mother Theodore Guérin of the Religious of the Sacred Heart. In a letter to her French superior she notes:

> I am not sure whether I told you of the insupportable pride of the Americans. When dinner time came, there was my washerwoman sitting down at table with us. I was so indiscreet as to say it would be better for her not to take her dinner with the Community. I wish you could have seen the change in the countenances of our American postulants! . . . The mere name of 'servant' makes them revolt, and they throw down whatever they have in their hands and start off at once.[21]

Noting the difference between the values of European religious life and those on which Americans were nurtured, Mother Guérin assumed that prospective religious would have to give up their American values. This expectation is consistent with the spirituality described above as typical of the period. American energy and independence were being challenged through religious life to meet the needs of the church of the day, but at a price.

How were these religious received?

One might wonder whether a life chosen at so high a price was valued. In the ante-bellum period the climate of the day had become hostile to Catholics for a variety of reasons. Protestant revivalism contributed to the mood. Hostility to immigrants (especially Irish) was joined to the dislocations of early industrialization and urbanization. Anti-Catholic writing flourished, including wild tales of convent horrors. Sisters were noticeable by their garb and way of life. They frequently faced active animosity, ranging from petty harassment (like the Yale student who, on a bet, grabbed a sister and carried her for several blocks), through campaigns to deprive them of their livelihood by frightening away paying students, to the destruction of the Ursuline convent in Charleston.[22] Yet where sisters were known personally, whether through their nursing during epidemics or in their daily ministries, those who encountered them—Protestants as well as Catholics—respected and accepted them.[23] This was a harbinger of the shift in opinion to come during the Civil War.

THE IMMIGRANT CHURCH: THE WAR DECADE, 1860–1870

A major shift affects the situation of religious in the local church during this decade. Rather than address the guiding questions, it will be more helpful simply to examine this shift. There was a vast improvement in the public attitude toward sisters (and indirectly, toward Catholics) as a result of the work of the sister-nurses during the Civil War. Hennessey gives the statistics:

> between five and six hundred sisters from more than twenty religious communities were nurses in military hospitals. Outstanding were the Emmitsburg Daughters of Charity with two hundred and thirty-two nursing sisters.

He continues:

Sister Mary Agnes Kelly left a vivid description of the hospital at Pensacola, Florida, where she and others worked with soldiers suffering from tropical fever and measles as well as war wounds. Some had never before seen a Catholic sister: "When we went into the wards they covered their heads with the blankets and nothing would induce them to uncover them while we were in the wards for three or four days, as they were frightened by our appearance."[24]

Ewens summarizes the evidence that actual contact with sisters by the armies of both sides was effective in overcoming the negativity of the prewar decades.[25]

This is approximately the halfway point in the American story. Where were the religious in the local church? Religious were serving in a variety of ways at the request of superiors. Congregations first undertook specific works on their own initiative, but increasingly as time passed the initiative became the prerogative of the bishops. Sisters were teaching and nursing; running orphanages, schools, and hospitals; and doing domestic work. They were working with whites, with blacks, with Indians, and with Hispanics. The vast majority were with whites, reflecting the impetus given their work by the needs of a large and still steadily growing immigrant community.

THE IMMIGRANT CHURCH: THE EXPLOSIVE GROWTH OF 1870–1920

Who were the religious and what was expected of them?

What religious women were in this period is what superiors, directed by the bishops, judged the religious needed to be to serve the needs of the mushrooming Catholic immigrant population. Schools were the imperative—schools to teach the elements of the faith and, for some, schools to teach in the language of the community of ethnic origin.[26] In the 1850s and 1860s the public-school movement had been growing rapidly. Bible reading formed an important component of a

public-school education. Catholics objected to having their
children read the Protestant Bible. Protestant clergy rallied to
the defense of the public schools as central to the religious
education of American youth and criticized Catholic oppo-
nents. At the First Council of Baltimore in 1852 the bishops
encouraged parochial schools as the Catholic response. The
issue became political in the 1870s with Republicans against
tax support for schools under the control of religious organizations. The Third Council of Baltimore in 1884 devoted a
quarter of its legislation to schools. Two key points were the
directive that a school should be built near the church in
every parish, and the command to Catholic parents to send
their children to these schools.

One group of bishops, led by Archbishop John Ireland of St.
Paul, sought compromises for working with the public
schools. Ireland's hope was to build a bridge between the
American and Roman Catholic cultures. His work was in the
tradition of Archbishop Carroll, but it was counter to its own
time. The opposition, led by Bishop Bernard McQuaid of
Rochester, saw the school as a fortress. What he wanted were
walls to protect children from the "wolves of the world," who
were "destroying countless numbers of the unguarded ones";
consequently, "if the walls are not high enough, they must be
raised; if they are not strong enough, they must be strength-
ened."[27] As Dolan remarks, "a clearer statement of the Catholic fortress mentality would be hard to find." The outcome of
the debate was unclear. Ireland's plan failed in his own diocese. In fact, the Catholic schools never had the total support
of bishops or people. The problem was money; schools are
expensive, although the cost of teachers was not the problem
in this case.

Teachers were an absolute prerequisite for the schools, and
the vast majority of those teachers were religious women.
Their numbers had grown from 1,344 in 1850 to 40,340 by
1900. The extraordinary numbers and the willingness of the
community members to work for low wages made the Catholic
parochial schools possible.

Sisters had been teaching in academies and in schools for

the poor from the nation's earliest years. Nonetheless, the parochial school brought a different dimension to their work. In the years before 1900 some hope was expressed for a Catholic college for women, but its advocates rightly felt that the cloister regulations of the day precluded sisters having the proper training.

How were religious accepted?

During these years the church itself first recognized persons under simple vows as true religious. As I mentioned earlier, canonical norms changed in 1900 with the papal bull *Conditae a Christo*. The bull mitigated some of the prescriptions of cloister for active sisters, but it also restricted the kinds of work such sisters might do. Lest they endanger their vocations, sisters were not to care for babies, nurse maternity cases, manage clerical seminaries, or staff coeducational schools. The underlying view of women was still that of the weaker sex who must be protected. The Code of Canon Law of 1917 affirmed the recognition of status, but its specific legislation came close to delineating a "generic brand" of religious life, so that communities were in danger of losing their differing charisms.

While the public highly valued religious teachers and nurses just after the Civil War, the religious lost a certain amount of public esteem as the years went by. There were several reasons for this. Throughout the period, training for teachers improved but sisters whose rules forbade them to attend classes were unable to participate in it. They were restricted to the mentor system, and their training suffered. Foreign-born sisters were criticized for their lack of knowledge of English. As teaching was being professionalized, so too was nursing. Since many sisters could not participate in the training, they lost their leading position in the field.

The root of a number of the difficulties faced by religious was connected with the meaning of being an American. After all, can an immigrant be an American? Can a Catholic be an American? Can an immigrant Catholic—let alone an immigrant Catholic sister—be an American? The effort of a number

of bishops and priests to enculturate Catholicism in America
came to an end with the Roman condemnation of Americanism in 1899. As William Halsey has indicated, individuals
"were accused of heresy for espousing the activist individualism, self-confident mystique and optimistic idealism of
American civilization."[28] They were guilty of cultural difference, a condition somewhat different from heresy. What
was lost was the driving force in the movement to let Catholicism show an American face.

Rome launched a similar condemnation of Modernism in
1907, condemning a variety of positions dependent on
historical-critical biblical scholarship. The condemnation was
followed by what Hennessey has called "a thoroughgoing and
immensely effective educational police action."[29] The combination of the Americanist and the Modernist crises effectively ended for fifty years the development of authentically
American Catholic thought.

At the local level the consequences of the condemnations
appeared as staunch loyalty to the positions of the distinctively
Roman church. While Catholics often claimed to be both
totally Catholic and totally American, their fellow citizens
found this position hard to understand. The Catholic de-
meanor of certainty and of apartness did not help. Religious
sisters with their distinctive garb and way of life were more
apart than most.

FROM GHETTO TO MAINSTREAM, 1920–60

What was the sense of church?

The conviction of being right vis-à-vis the Protestant world
marked the American Catholic church in these decades. To be
a Catholic was to know the truth and to be charged with
protecting it against a world set on destroying it. The external
signs of Catholicism supported a piety rooted in devotional
practices. Meatless Fridays, Sunday Masses, and Lenten fasts
were but initial steps. Novenas, First Fridays, scapulars,

medals, and rosaries multiplied. They nourished a parallel, separate Catholic life intent on proving it was equal to whatever America had to offer. There was not only a Catholic parochial-school system but there were also Catholic sports leagues, a Catholic press, Catholic men's societies and women's clubs, Catholic scout troops and, of course, a guide to "decent movies." The effort to adapt religion to the culture had been aborted. Instead, culture was to be converted to religion. The ideal was to build a new society in which religion and life were integrated. The Catholic faith supported by the Catholic Thomistic philosophy would be effective. The church triumphant faced the world through boom and depression. One's viewpoint would determine whether it looked out from a fortress or a ghetto.

The flow of foreign-born Catholics had been cut off with the immigration restrictions of 1924. Through the post-World War II years, nonetheless, the population boomed.[30] The same years saw record numbers of vocations and vast church building programs to accommodate the numbers. The move to the suburbs and the influx of blacks and Hispanics into previously white areas of the country also changed the situation of the Catholic church by the end of the period. Furthermore, the G.I. Bill not only made education available to millions of veterans, but it also changed the schools that educated these men and hastened the mainstreaming of Catholics. A period which began with the defeat of Al Smith's presidential campaign ended with the election of John F. Kennedy as Catholics began to move from the ghetto to the mainstream.

Who were the religious and what was expected of them?

The burgeoning of the Catholic high schools and the multiplication of Catholic colleges occurred in the 1920s through the 1940s. Religious sisters taught at both levels. The parochial school, however, remained the key to the Catholic school system. The movement for certification of teachers gained momentum after World War I. Coupled with the work of the accrediting agencies, it began to put pressure on teachers in the Catholic schools to improve professional preparation. The movement further burdened sisters already responsible for large classes, after-school catechism classes for public-school children, and their own religious obligations. In the 1950s Pius XII confirmed this direction, calling on religious communities, and especially sisters, to improve the education of their members. The Sister Formation movement was influential in educating sisters so that increasingly they were degreed before stepping into the classroom. The improvement in the education of sisters is one of two significant steps taken to change the situation of women religious in the last seven hundred years. The other is the successful foundation of the Daughters of Charity without cloister.

How were the religious received?

The numbers drawn to the life tell a story. In 1954 there were 158,069 religious sisters, increasing to 181,421 in the peak year of 1965. It is clear that within the Catholic community the religious vocation was valued and respected. In the broader community, things Catholic, including Catholic religious, enjoyed the general regard in which religion was held during the 1950s. National figures like Bishop Fulton J. Sheen and the Trappist monk Thomas Merton engaged the attention and won the respect of the wider American populace.

CONCLUSION

Where were religious in the local church at the close of this survey? Interestingly, in 1960 ministries remained fundamentally unchanged. Sisters taught, nursed, and did social work. Unchanged, too, was the structure by which direct obedience to a superior placed the individual religious in a work.

In the young Republic the church led by John Carroll tried to incorporate the American values of independence from foreign control, democratic process, and respect for religious pluralism. It developed the germ of a presbyteral model. The church envisioned itself as standing *with* the American culture. As the nineteenth century progressed, the pressures of immigration and urbanization changed the climate in America. All the churches became less democratic and more hierarchical. Growing papal authority accentuated the trend to hierarchical control in Catholicism. The church increasingly saw itself as standing *against* the American culture. At the beginning of the twentieth century, the combined crises of Americanism and Modernism intensified the "fortress" or "ghetto" mentality of Catholics in the United States. It was only in the years following World War II that Catholics began to enter the mainstream of American life in significant numbers. Pressure was building for the church to rethink its position as *within* the modern world rather than against it, and so *within* and *of* the American culture, and not apart from that culture. This marked the dawn of the day whose full light saw publication of the Pastoral Constitution on the Church in the Modern World and the Declaration on Religious Freedom.

Religious were affected by the same forces. Religious women, while still hampered by numerous cloistral restrictions, profited from advanced education. They remained Americans. Despite Mother Theodore Guérin's early hope, it no longer seemed possible to eliminate American values to make good religious. Soon it would no longer be thought necessary. American independence, American trust in democratic process, and American respect for pluralism were waiting in the vestibule, seeking admission to religious life in the 1960s. The end of this chapter is the opening of one of the most challenging and interesting volumes in the history of religious life. That will be the story of the true universalizing of the church, as it—and religious life—become truly at home in each of the world's cultures. For American Catholics that story begins in the United States as they continue to seek to become, in the spirit of John Carroll, a fully enculturated American church in union with Rome.

4

U.S. Ecclesial Women, 1960–1985

For ecclesial women living and working in the Catholic church in the United States between 1960 and 1985 the experience of change was seriously affected by the nation's turmoil during those years, and governed by Vatican II's mandate to renew religious congregations. The 1960s opened with the election of John F. Kennedy as the first Catholic President of the United States. In the turbulent years before and after his assassination in 1963, American self-consciousness was redefined by the civil-rights movement and the women's movement. In the early 1970s the country's psyche was scarred by the Vietnam war. The Watergate scandal completed the despoliation of whatever political innocence remained. Ecclesial women were active participants in civil-rights work as well as the women's movement and the peace movement. Many chose to walk the picket lines, to march, to engage in boycotts, and to perform various acts of resistance to the war. Entire congregations reexamined their call to the faith that does justice and positioned themselves on the side of the weak and the politically oppressed.

Simultaneously, dating from 1965, all congregations were mandated by the Second Vatican Council to engage in a process of renewal by returning to the scriptures and to the original inspiration of their institutes, and adapting to the changed conditions of the times.[1] The first step required each congregation to hold a general chapter of renewal leading to the review of the constitutions which form the principal governing document of each group.[2] In general American religious women responded enthusiastically to this challenge. The first visible effects were changes in dress, followed quickly by changes in schedule, in forms of community and personal prayer, and in works. Here the American qualities of freedom, independence, and pluralism quickly became more evident as ecclesial women rethought religious life and sought to find the best correlation between the Gospels, the founding charisms of their various groups, and the American situation. Nonetheless at this time there was a 31 percent drop in membership in women's religious communities, a phenomenon which will be considered in more detail in chapter 5.

The women's movement affected the process, especially after the publication of *Humanae Vitae* (Paul VI's papal encyclical on birth control) in 1968 and of the declaration of the Sacred Congregation for the Doctrine of the Faith *On the Question of the Admission of Women to the Ministerial Priesthood* in 1976. Positions taken about sexuality and women in the ministerial priesthood concern all women. In particular, many women religious, all of whom seek to be truly ecclesial women, found themselves experiencing internal conflict with church teaching while simultaneously undergoing the process of renewal within their congregations.

The attempt to resolve these matters with integrity has been fraught with difficulty. The fundamental issue requires examination.

ARE WOMEN INFERIOR IN THE CHURCH?

The nature of women and the place of women in the church are the underlying questions. In Galatians 3:27–28 Paul affirms there is but one baptism, there is but one Christ, in whom human beings are neither slave nor free, neither Gentile nor Jew, neither woman nor man. The Apostle speaks of the way in which, through the one common baptism and faith, all distinctions among human beings are erased. Next, Paul articulates the same reality in a different mode of thought. According to Galatians 4 all have become participants in the life of the Spirit, a life won by Christ, God's Son born of a woman, a life in which human beings share on the model of the children of Sarah, Abraham's freeborn wife. There are neither distinctions in baptism nor in the life of the Spirit. Just as all the daughters and sons of Sarah share equally in her freedom, so all who live the life of the Spirit share equally in the Spirit's freedom. It is, however, a symptom of the current problem that the importance of the text has itself been frequently overlooked. The neglect leads to arguments *favoring* slavery, *against* Jews, and *in favor of* the subjection of women. The radical equality of all in Christ Jesus has not been universally welcomed as "good news."[3]

Yet church teaching is that the baptized are children of God, heirs of heaven, and temples of the Holy Spirit. All are baptized with the same water, anointed with the same chrism and with the same formula.[4] It ought therefore to be simply a rhetorical question to ask if the effects of baptism are the same for all, or if they apply to men only, or to men more than women. What is at issue has to do with women's nature as women, and so this is an issue of theological anthropology. It is a question of women and the place of women in the church. Concretely the questions become: Are women equal to men, or are there distinctions, and if so, what are the distinctions? Before considering theoretical answers to these questions, it will be well to consider women's experience.

REVIEW OF WOMEN'S EXPERIENCE

The experiences of three different women are instructive. Their names are fictitious, but their stories are true. Meet Ann—bright, single, in her early thirties. She holds three advanced degrees: a master's in pastoral counseling, a master's of divinity, and a licentiate in theology. She is repaying her student loans while supporting herself on her salary as an associate pastor in a Midwestern parish. She is properly hired by a pastor to do a task within her competence. She prepares people for the sacraments, gives instructions, visits the sick, and takes annulment testimony. She wants that job right now, because it is a good fit with her sense of vocation to serve the church as a lay minister. Ann speaks of deanery meetings where she is the only woman, tolerated because of her competence and the support of her pastor, but not welcomed. However, this clerical tolerance is in some ways easier to deal with than the resistance of the people, to whom she must prove her competence and who do not recognize her authority. Apparently what is happening here is the recognition by both clerics and laity that Ann is outside the power structure; because she is, she lacks authority. The structures of ministry in the Roman Catholic church accommodate the lay minister only with difficulty. It is interesting that as people accept her, they most usually call Ann "sister." She is a laywoman, not a religious. Will conversion of heart of the individuals involved be enough to change the situation of the lay minister in the future, or is structural change necessary? What is called for by reflection on this experience in the light of the gospel?

Betty is another single laywoman and is in her early forties. On completion of her master's of divinity, Betty was accepted by Maryknoll for further training as a lay missioner. The class she joined there consisted of single laywomen and men, as well as married couples. She will soon be at her post in Central America. Betty supported herself throughout her education. In a time of vocation shortages, it is interesting to note that Maryknoll continues to send out a steady stream of missioners. The makeup of the groups, however, has shifted from exclusively sisters, brothers, and priests to include single and married laypeople. The picture is not unlike that of the diverse group of coworkers of Paul identified in Romans 16. Women in the missions (e.g., think of the slain Jean Donovan and her companions), report no problem in acceptance. The structure supporting them *has* been changed. Maryknoll is prepared to accept these women and men as coworkers and to train them. The people in mission territories are prepared to receive missioners with various life commitments. Is this not a model for revision of structures of ministry?

Meet Caroline, an M.A. candidate in her mid-twenties. Caroline's goal is to teach in Catholic schools, eventually as a married woman. Despite the "call of the whole church to holiness"[5] by Vatican II, Caroline sees the married status as "second class" in the church. In her view, really to belong to the club, one must be single, and preferably a priest or sister. The problem for Caroline is a structural one. The married are outside all decision-making structures and without any authority. Only celibates are "inside" the system. (Many sisters would argue that it is not enough to be vowed celibates. One must be male.) Contemporary experience calls for adults to take appropriate responsibility for the actions of the groups in which they are involved; to give over all responsibility, as a child would to a parent, is inappropriate. Both employees and students have appropriate involvement in decisions affecting their work and studies. To be part of the family of Christ does not mean acceptance of the status of perpetual childhood. The question is at root a question of the nature of personhood. Here it is also a question about the nature of the church. What does it mean to be an adult in the church, whether celibate, single, or married? And what does the perceived second-class status of the married say about the church's view of sex and matrimony?

Notice that Ann, Betty, and Caroline are women involved in experiences which at one level could just as well be those of men. The difference is that they are women trying to engage as equals in a male-oriented church. Though still exceptional, the numbers of such women are growing both within the church and in society at large. It remains true that there are large numbers of women in the church content with their situation, although perhaps disturbed by a particular issue.

In the larger society, however, the picture is somewhat different. For a growing minority, women's experience is the experience of poverty.[6] Two out of every three poor adults in this country are women. A 1981 study concluded that if the current trend continues at the same rate, "the poverty population would be composed solely of women and their children before the year 2000."[7] The following random statistics tell their own tale:

It takes a woman nine days of fulltime labor on the average to earn what a man makes in five days.

Black mothers who work full time, year-round, have a poverty rate of 13 percent, the same rate as white men who do not work at all.

Minority women are most likely to work in the lowest paid of all women's jobs and to experience the most extreme poverty of all.

If wives and female heads of households were paid the same as similarly qualified men, half the families now living in poverty would not be poor.

Only 6 out of every 100 working women ever make it to management.

Women with a college education earn less, on the average, than men with only a high-school diploma.

The situation is precipitated by the sexist structures of the private economy, reinforced by federal, state, and city governments. It is not an unrelated phenomenon that Ann, Betty, and Caroline each financed their preparation for ministry in the church themselves. Minimal support for preparation for lay ministry continues in the church just as its support for retired sisters has been almost nonexistent.[8] Reflection on this current experience of women in the light of the gospel demands structural change. The human dignity of women and the requirements of justice demand this. The experience of women, both in the larger society and in the church, is one of separation and nonequality. The difficulty in the church is that there is no coherence between baptismal theology and daily life. Theory does not impact on praxis.

THE NATURE OF WOMEN

There are two commonly used and readily distinguishable answer to the question of women's nature. The first says women and men are radically different. The second says

women and men are equal, although advocates of this model
may qualify the equality in various ways. To understand the
models it helps to see them at work. The question "What is
woman?" was addressed with explicit attention to the two
models in the dialogue on women in the church held between
representatives of the Women's Ordination Conference and
the National Conference of Catholic Bishops. Six sessions of
the dialogue took place between December 1979, and August
1981.[9] The nature of women was the topic for the fourth
session.[10]

Anne Carr's article on theological anthropology and
women's experience[11] was a key resource for the participants.
In it Carr states that there are three models concerning
human nature and women: two-nature, one-nature, and transformational. In fact, the transformational reduces to a version
of the one-nature model, so there are but the two models. In
the two-nature model, women and men are recognized as
different, having opposite natures and roles: man-public,
woman-private; man-work, woman-home, etc. It is such an
opinion that underlay the 1917 Code of Canon Law, in which
women were grouped with children. In that case the difference implies inferiority. (It might be helpful to note that
the operative definition of nature here seems to be a collection
of characteristics or attributes. It is judged that women and
men have different characteristics or attributes; thus, they
must have different natures.)

In more recent writings, the term "complementary" is
used. This appears in another resource used by the dialogue,
the intervention of the American bishops in the synod at
Rome in 1980.[12] There the bishops affirmed that

> Co-equality, interdependence and complementarity of men
> and women in marriage and in the institutions of society are
> the will of God. It is a fact that major tasks in society—
> government, medicine, education, religion, child-rearing—
> can be best accomplished by men and women in co-equal and
> complementary cooperation and partnership.[13]

One must ask whether "complementary" here means "separate but equal" (which easily slips over into "separate and inferior"), or whether it is an affirmation of ontological equality. The difficulty is that when affirmations of ontological equality do not lead to operational equality, the sincerity of the affirmations becomes suspect. This was the opinion of women participating in the dialogue. They stated:

> It is felt by many women . . . that the operative assumption out of which teaching is promulgated is the notion of un-efficacious complementarity, i.e., that women are subordinate.[14]

After discussion the women and bishops together agreed to this statement about the issue of complementarity:

> Church documents imply that complementarity and equality are compatible terms. Historically the term complementarity has meant a differentiation of men and women according to different sets of innate, personal qualities which has the effect of assigning men and women to separate and unequal roles and spheres. While it was supposed to suggest harmonious diversity, in practice the notion of complementarity actually results in dominant-dependent roles based on sex in the church and society. In view of the above, the dialoguers urge the use of a term more indicative of the mutuality of persons.[15]

Thus the discussants agreed that the languages of complementarity and of equality are not compatible.

The second model views women and men as having the same nature. It denies rigidly defined roles for women and men other than biological. Characteristics of the *individual* then become determinative of all other roles. (Here nature is taken to denote a concrete existent individual. Women and men are each that in the same way, in this view.) The goal set for the one-nature anthropology is that "either sex can and should develop those qualities traditionally associated with the other."[16] A certain kind of androgyny is thus anticipated.

In practice, men define this nature, and characteristics commonly associated with men are preferred for leadership positions: cool rationality, assertiveness, courage, strength, etc. Thus there occur such anomalies as Queen Elizabeth I identifying herself as "prince." Ordinarily, the situation has resulted in women being excluded from leadership roles. Participants in the dialogue, reflecting on this model, remarked that women and men may have the same nature, but the dominant elite, the men who have the power, define that nature.[17]

The transformational model is a variation on the two-nature one. Developed by Mary Buckley,[18] it aims at transforming the old gender stereotypes at the same time as it seeks to transform the social and cultural structures that are their context in human life. Buckley sees the two-nature model correlated with the hierarchical organization of society in the nation-state. The one-nature model correlates with the postrevolutionary egalitarian state. In this model, the ideals of democracy mask the real ruling group, a group which in America excludes blacks, Indians, newly arrived immigrants, and women. The true paradigm is the upper elite, which in America consists of white males, usually Protestant. Thus the one-nature model, as well as the two-nature model, can be used to support the traditional inferior status of women.

Buckley argues that if this condition is to change, both traditionally female and traditionally male qualities are needed to perform a radical critique of social institutions as well as of individuals. When participants in the dialogue reflected on this model, at least as the discussion was reported, they missed this point and so overlooked the distinctive element of the model. The report simply mentions that, according to this model, women can develop masculine qualities and men feminine. No attention was given to social criticism leading to the transformation of social structures. This is Buckley's major contribution. The one-nature model for understanding women as persons equal with men needs to be joined to a critique of social structures if it is to be future-oriented rather than past-confirming.

As a result of the dialogue bishop participants listed as

learnings: (1) many women experience alienation within the church because of sexism; (2) there is inconsistency between the church's teaching on justice in civil society and its practice of justice toward its own members; (3) church language about complementarity can involve implied subordination of women. Finally, the bishops said they found a new understanding of patriarchy. They wrote:

> In our dialogue about an authoritative apostolic ministry given by Jesus to the church we were confronted with a new perspective. Does the hierarchical nature of the church necessarily have to be patriarchal?[19]

It was their study of the scriptures and of the egalitarian nature of the early church that bishop participants found most helpful in bringing them to this insight. But the whole question of the nature of women as persons remained as unfinished business at the completion of the dialogue.

TWO MODELS AND THEIR CONSEQUENCES FOR CHANGE

That unfinished business surfaced again in the national hearings for the bishops' letter on women. Participants in the hearings at all levels were asked to consider the conditions that contribute to the alienation of women, the conditions that contribute to the reconciliation of women, and the issues or themes important for the development of such a pastoral. In the case of each testifying group analysis reveals the model at work together with certain methodological factors proper to each model. The next part of this chapter is an examination of the reports of the national hearings, uncovering the correlation among model, methodology, and whether a group's feminism leads it to social critique ("higher criticism") or to issue critique ("lower criticism").[20] Ten groups participated in the hearings.[21] Basic to the positions of four groups[22] is a two-nature anthropology, while the majority appeared to work from a one-nature anthropology. In each case, while not explicit, the chosen model reveals itself to analysis.

For example, testimony of the Catholic Daughters of America affirms that its members "welcome the acceptance of women as having equal capabilities."[23] It then states that women thrust into the workplace "do not seek to compete with men" but "yearn to be accepted as equal or simply as complementary to their male co-workers."[24] This is a reflection of the two-nature model. To it is joined a recognition of the change made by Jesus in recognizing women's humanity, of present change, for example, that forced on women by the economy, and that made by the new Code of Canon Law. Call for structural change is absent. In its place the testimony pledges "We are women loyal to the tenets of the church and accept the judgments and decrees of the Holy Father."[25] One group, the Consortium Perfectae Caritatis, explicitly affirms the CDA statement in its own testimony.[26]

Similar positions are assumed by the National Conference of Catholic Women. Their testimony affirms that the typically masculine and feminine characteristics are rooted in physiology. Masculine logic and feminine intuition together can interpret the word of God more fully. Thus the NCCW testifies that

> just as the mutality of men and women within the family creates and forms well-functioning human beings, with men and women's gifts exercised in harmonious relationship, also the men and women of the church can blend their gifts in mutuality to make manifest the church as a compelling instrument of God's love.[27]

Here the two-nature model is combined with the language of complementarity. The testimony calls for a wide range of changes, from expansion of ministries for women within the church to seeking justice for abused and violated women within society. At the same time it makes a firm profession of faith "that the teaching authority of the church was commissioned by Christ to the apostolic succession which is guided by the Holy Spirit to make known the Christian message in every age."[28] Structural criticism plays no part in this testimony.

In the testimony of Women for Faith and Family, structural criticism is explicitly rejected.[29] This group prefers not to speak of the alienation or needed reconciliation of women since it finds the categories untrue. If it must use them, WFF holds that what contributes to the alienation of women is those conditions and attitudes in our culture "which lead women to forget their own distinct nature as beings made in God's image."[30] The positive claim about women's nature is that it is linked psychically and physically to maternity and so to children.[31] Further reflections on the implications of women's nature are based on various magisterial writings. Likewise, women's ordination is to be rejected as in conflict with the constant teaching of the church, further developed by recent magisterial statements. The problem of sexist language could be resolved by use of the teaching office to bring the church to a better understanding of "the distinctiveness and complementarity of the sexes which is part of the divine plan for humanity."[32]

There is some methodological agreement among these groups. All depend heavily on teaching authority uncritically received. All assume a revelation definitively given in the past. Teaching authority is expected to proclaim that revelation today. These groups understand women as created other than men and complementary to men. There is little if any sense that present experience is to be reflected on in the light of the scriptures precisely in order that *new* insight might come for the future. New or radically other possibilities for women's existence are precluded. At the same time all these groups take seriously the present plight of women. While evil in some form is named as causative of that plight, none link women's plight to structural or systemic evil. The problem is rooted in women's choices or in society; it is seldom located in the church itself. All these groups thus practice "lower criticism." They prefer to concern themselves with separate issues affecting women and not with structural causes.

The case is different with those groups who follow the one-nature model. The testimony of the Leadership Conference of Women Religious, followed by the Association of Contemplative Sisters, is illustrative. Women are identified as engaged in a movement toward recognizing themselves as "possessing inherent dignity and worth" which leads to "insistence that others relate to them, both personally and structurally, in ways that affirm that dignity." This can lead to relationships with men "in which there are mutual support and respect and peer-to-peer sharing."[33] At the same time, the document states:

> the church lacks a strong tradition regarding the equality and basic dignity and worth of women. In contrast to its distinguished history of both thought and experience regarding war and peace, and economic justice . . . there is no comparable ground in which a pastoral on women can be rooted.[34]

This is clear evidence of a one-nature anthropology. To it is joined an explicit call for structural change. The alienation of women (i.e., the identification of women as alien, other, and not as one with or equal) is traced to patriarchy. Patriarchy is defined as a world-view which

> places the male in the center of reality and makes the masculine normative. It defines and structures relationships— whether personal or systemic—in terms of dominance and subservience and images all realities—from the deity to the mineral—in higher/lower rank. In such a world order women cannot be anything but inferior; they must of necessity be judged deficient since, if the male/masculine is the normative, they are different (abnormal). Where patriarchy as a world view is operative, symbols and rituals, relationships, structures and laws, definitions of identity, express, reinforce and perpetuate fundamental inequality.[35]

This world-view must be replaced by affirmation of the basic equality of all if human beings are to experience the world as a community of equal persons. The group clearly practices "higher criticism." Structural change is called for, including change in worship, in language, in church polity, and in the ways in which clergy and hierarchy approach public-policy questions affecting women.

The other four groups hold similar positions with varying emphases. Marriage Encounter argued strongly for equality and for structural changes to enable that equality. In their view, women are not the problem; rather it is the understanding of personhood which is at issue. [36] They were supported in this position by the North American Conference of Separated and Divorced Catholics, who see the problem not as women but as patriarchy and sexism. [37] The Committee on the Laity, noting the exit of men as women move into their once exclusive professions, contributed the question: "What are men running from?"[38] The Women's Ordination Conference introduced a methodological departure. Its testimony took the form of a parable invoking prophetic imagination.

Methodologically, the testimony of the groups supporting the one-nature anthropology have more similarities than differences. The departure point for all groups is the current experience of women. Gospel freedom is the yardstick by which that experience is measured. The assumption is that women's future can and should be different from the past. Structural changes are called for to bring about a situation of radical equality like that named in Galatians.

There is a strong resemblance between the methodologies correlative to each of the two anthropologies and the methodologies correlative to the two positions in the debate on religious freedom at Vatican II. One need but recall John Courtney Murray's study "The Problem of Religious Freedom."[39] The methodology of the group supporting the one-nature anthropology is very like that of the group supporting religious freedom and like that adopted in *Gaudium et Spes*. This methodology proceeds by reflection on present experience (the "signs of the times"), and permits the gospel to illuminate that experience, in the process bringing church teaching "up to date."[40] Supporters of the one-nature anthropology follow this method favored in the Council. They work from experience in the light of the gospel and advocate change in previous teaching to implement a future situation more in accord with gospel principles. The expectation is that individuals and structures must be changed to effect significant differences. Supporters of the two-nature anthropology work from previous teaching and advocate change in the present situation of women to effect an experience more in accord with the gospel. The expectation is that individuals must change to effect significant differences.

The first draft of the pastoral *Partners in the Mystery of Redemption* offers an example of incomplete adoption of the one-nature anthropology. In strong sections on person and on society the bishops reject sexism and apply the principles of social justice to issues affecting women. The rejection of sexism is valuable in two respects. It represents a new evaluation of much of the tradition and, because this new evaluation is rooted theologically in the incarnation of Christ, it calls attention to the theological basis of woman's equality in personhood. The bishops affirm that Christ condemned sexism by his coming in *human* likeness. The bishops' argument against sexism is based not only on the direct teaching of Christ but also on the very humanity of Christ.

In the debate around women's ordination it is the maleness (rather than the humanity) of Christ that has been claimed as decisive if the priest is to act truly *in persona Christi*. By contrast, a constant and central Christian teaching has been that it is by virtue of Christ's *humanity* that *all humans* are saved. The patristic enunciation of the principle is that what was "assumed" (or "taken on" in the incarnation) is what was saved. When the maleness of Christ becomes doctrinally central, one must logically ask if and how women are saved. The approach here, although it is not at all in the context of the ordination discussion, employs the christological argument in a more sober fashion wholly in keeping with the main line of the tradition. Women are equals in personhood with men. The very person of Christ, who has become *human,* condemns as sinful the denigration of one sex by the other.

When this declaration moves to the area of relationships

there is no fresh approach to the underlying problem of sexuality. In this area positions established before retain overwhelming authority. Similarly, when discussing women in the church, the bishops call for study of the admission of women to the diaconate and for their admission to various lay ministries. Nonetheless they ask for continued study of women's ordination to the priesthood since such study "could help to place in the proper light the church's consistent practice."[41] The authority of previous practice and decisions not only precludes the possibility of ordination to the priesthood but also shapes the kind of study of the question for which the bishops call.

A consistent adoption of the one-nature anthropology ought to be joined to a critique of structures. When facing the theoretical question of the nature of women or the situation of women in society the bishops in the first draft call for structural change. However, when facing either matters of sexuality on which the church has firm received positions, or matters of internal church organization fixed by past practice, the framers of the first draft revert to single-issue change. It is true that the role of tradition in church teaching and practice must be taken into account. However, fidelity to the gospel requires a procedure more in line with that followed at Vatican II, in which traditional teachings and practice are also submitted to scrutiny in the light of that gospel and contemporary conditions.

CONCLUSION

There are a number of insights that can be drawn from this analysis: (1) Women's experience of society is the experience of the economically marginated and (2) women's experience of the church, for many, is the experience of an inferior, one who has limited personal autonomy and value. (3) The issue is the personhood of women. Within the church, it is a question of the meaning of baptismal equality. (4) Those who subscribe to the two-nature anthropology interpret baptismal equality as complementary with separate roles for women and men. "Complementarity" often masks the assumption of the inferiority of women. In practice, the two-nature anthropology works from acceptance of past teaching by preferring to deal with issues one by one. (5) In contrast those who subscribe to the one-nature anthropology interpret baptismal equality as identity of nature, with characteristics of the individual determining roles. In practice, the one-nature anthropology works from analysis of present experience in light of the gospel. It prefers to engage in structural critique. (6) Deeper and more extensive change depends on implementation of structural change. However, a church which seriously considers its historical roots cannot simply "forget" its past. Recollection of past teaching, and critical growth from it, will remain part of Catholic practice. Attention to single issues can force church members to engage their past in ways that bring the gospel alive in the present. Ultimately this type of activity will lead to more radical criticism if permanent growth is to ensue. Therefore the two processes, lower and higher criticism, nurture each other.

5

A Focused Witness

In the contemporary situation women's societal experience is all too often that of the economically marginated, and many ecclesial women experience their position as that of inferiors. The number of religious women has shrunk drastically. There was so great an exodus from religious life between 1965 and 1980 that in 1981 there were 31 percent fewer sisters than in 1966.[1] The Pontifical Commission on Religious Life was established by Pope John Paul II in 1983 explictly to study the reasons for the declining numbers.[2] The reasons are not yet fully understood. Examination of the situation reveals that something new is appearing in the lives of American religious women. That new thing is a more focused witness with a specific emphasis on the life of celibacy in the context of community. The particular community context involves the ideal of leadership as a mutual responsibility. This will be examined in chapter 6. Here the subject is the relationship between fewer numbers and the emphasis on celibacy.

Factors affecting the decline in numbers include the societal situation, the situation of the church and of women religious within the church, and the situation of potential candidates. After these have been reviewed it is possible to discern the relationship between the shrunken number of religious and the particular emphasis or gift proper to active religious women today. Some time ago, I invited women and men in various parts of the country to join in my reflection on factors that influence the decision to enter religious life today. I have quoted some of their remarks in what follows.

SOCIETAL FACTORS AFFECTING THE ENTRY RATE

It is a given that culture opposes the values that religious
life stands for. This has consistently been the case in the
history of religious life and is not new. However, there are
three specific societal factors that appear to affect choice today. The nuclear issue is critical. Reflective young adults ask:
"Is there to be a normal lifetime?" "Can I expect to live out
the decade?" Evidently for some the response to the threat of
nuclear catastrophe is a form of paralysis. It becomes impossible to plan a life-choice or to decide a lifework. A veteran in
his mid-thirties explains: "It's impossible to think of a normal
lifetime. It's too long. A year is OK; five years is a stretch. I
can't see beyond that." Yet some are impelled by similar
considerations to enter religious life. Their perspective on the
choice is provocative. A novice in her mid-twenties maintains:
"The only possible commitment is to peace. Anything else has
to come step by step. I can commit to the novitiate, then to
the next stage. I can't think farther." A society on the brink of
self-destruction offers its younger members little scope and
less motivation for long-range planning. How can religious
communities respond to such a dilemma? Possibly the only
useful response is dedication to the cause of peace and nuclear
disarmament. The American bishops indicated as much in
outlining the elements of a pastoral response to the dilemma
of our time.[3]

A second societal factor related to the nuclear issue, but
also found independently of reflection on that issue, is the
difficulty with permanent commitment. Process and change
are values in themselves in the United States in the late
twentieth century. This is evident in a marketplace geared to
disposability and replacement; in the expectation that occupa-
tional mobility is desirable; in the expectations of moving from
house to house, from county to county, even from state to
state; and in the rapidly escalating divorce rate with the
accompanying reconstitution of families. In this situation
merely to contemplate a permanent relationship to a religious

congregation is in itself already a countercultural stance. By contrast, limited commitment is attractive. It is useful to reflect on the implications of the flood of applications for the Jesuit International Volunteers. In the spring of 1985 there were eighty-five complete applications for twenty-two places; the twenty-two accepted completed training and are now in service. At the national level there are as of this writing 313 Jesuit Volunteers. The Southwest story is typical: 110 applied for sixty-two places. At a minimum, this reflects the willingness of young people to engage in direct, *short-term* service. ROTC enlistment is a related phenomenon and quite consistent with one interpretation of the nuclear issue. It has the added benefit of offering both educational and job training at a time when the young person needs both in the struggle toward self-identity. Congregations and dioceses need to consider a variety of ways to make available and appealing a temporary relationship.

A third societal factor is the benefits for women won through the feminist movement.[4] As women attain more equal education and as opportunities for achievement within the society open, however slowly, one attraction of religious life is removed. Religious life has made available careers and leadership opportunities otherwise not open to women. The life may not have been consciously chosen for these reasons, but that the life offered opportunities once not available elsewhere remains a fact. This pattern of particular opportunities available only through the religious life replicates on a smaller scale what is true on a larger scale of the life itself. In its origins and throughout its history, religious life has functioned as *the* alternative to marriage for Roman Catholic women.

Examination of the apocryphal writings of the second and third centuries (a body of the popular literature of the day) makes clear that the development of the choice of a life of religiously dedicated chastity was viewed as the development of a life-option for women opposed to the socially approved pattern of marriage.[5] Since the institutionalization of the monastic life in the late fourth century, the options available to women in the West have been marriage or religious life. As we have seen in earlier chapters, the monastic life itself was increasingly a cloistered life for women from the sixth century onward. Despite the efforts of laywomen like the Beguines, of the mendicant third orders, and of women concerned to live an apostolic life—women like Angela Merici and Mary Ward—the cloister or marriage remained the available options until the work of Vincent de Paul and Louise de Marillac in the seventeenth century. With their achievement, the options became cloister, service in the convent, or marriage. Even here, we saw that church legislation did not recognize women with simple vows as "religious" until 1900. At that time the impact of the work of women like Catherine McAuley was indirectly recognized.[6] Thus the cloister, the convent, or marriage remained the primary options for women until the last twenty-five years. With the opening of other opportunities to women, religious life has become less attractive.

FACTORS SITUATED WITHIN THE CHURCH

Religious life might not have become less attractive if it were not for a number of additional factors that are immediately situated within the church itself. Three of these factors are the emerging lay role, the institutional face of the church, and the situation of women religious in the church.

The emerging lay role

Here the terms "lay" and "laity" denote those members of the church who are neither clerics nor bound by public religious profession.[7] It is a common conviction that *the* crisis today is not one of religious vocations but rather one of the emergence of the lay vocation within the church. This has been shaped by the Vatican II decree on the laity, as well as by both the content and inclusion of the chapters on the laity and on the call of the whole church to holiness in the Council's Dogmatic Constitution on the Church. This conciliar emphasis is but the next development in a series easily traceable from the nineteenth century here and in Europe: the impact of papal teaching on social justice, the Knights of Labor in late nineteenth-century America, fraternal organizations like the Knights of Columbus, the Retreat movement, the Christian Family movement, the Catholic Action movement of the 1930s and 1940s, and the Liturgical movement, oriented toward development of the lay apostolate from the 1930s to the 1950s. Now, in the last decades of the twentieth century, laity are taking their place in catechesis, liturgical life, and the service ministries. Roles they fill are roles that religious and, in some cases, priests used to fill. After all, the call to minister in the church flows neither from religious profession nor from ordination but is part of the common call to discipleship and flows from baptism. The shift is in *who* ministers. The same public ministries are being performed. Now it is often a laywoman or a layman who performs them. This is a very credible phenomenon. In fact, one role for religious in the current situation is to facilitate this development. As one brother remarked: "We must decrease to permit them to increase. In relation to this development we will be and look different." The emerging lay role is a positive development within the church that has consequences for the phenomenon of religious life.

The Institutional face of the church

Lay leaders share with religious the encounter with the institutional face of the church. The face that the institutional church turns toward church members, as well as toward non-members, is a face whose lineaments are often hardened by clericalism and by the accompanying patriarchalism which is destructive of healthy relationships among adults, and in particular between women and men. In their 1983 study the Conference of Major Superiors of Men identified clericalism as

> . . . the conscious or unconscious concern to promote the
> particular interests of the clergy and to protect the privileges

and power that have traditionally been conceded to those in
the clerical state. . . . Among its chief manifestations are an
authoritarian style of leadership, a rigidly hierarchical world
view, and a virtual identification of the holiness and grace of
the church with the clerical state and, thereby, with the cleric
himself.[8]

This attitude is rooted in the social reality of patriarchal
culture which

. . . is characterized by several features: the institutionalization of male privilege and power and an accompanying social
mythology to account for it: the social and cultural inequality
of men and women and the assumption that this represents the
appropriate (even God-given) pattern for all social relationships: and the formation and legitimation of vertical structures of power that are based on the presumed superiority and
inferiority of given classes of people.[9]

The document points out that clericalism has clear connec-
tions with patriarchal culture in its assumptions about social
structures, the vertical lines of authority and power, and the
privileges of caste. Such a situation is destructive of the emergence of lay roles in the church. It is particularly harmful to
women in that it reinforces a subordinate and passive role for
women. The perception of the institutional church as clerical
and patriarchal, and so as male-biased and female-exploita-
tive, is a serious impediment facing gifted and independent
women considering a vocation to religious life in the church.

The situation of women religious in the church

As if the perception of the institutional church as clerical
and patriarchal were not enough with which to confront a
thoughtful woman, the situation of women's religious congregations vis-à-vis the institutional church in the last decade
must also be considered. Here again there are three neuralgic
areas: the process for approval of the constitutions of congregations, the handling of cases like those of the signers of
the *New York Times* ad, and the papal intervention in apos-

tolic religious life in the United States. In terms of the process for approval of constitutions, it is apparent to the thoughtful potential candidate that women have struggled for some years, at the behest of the Holy See,[10] to renew their congregations in an appropriate manner. The process for approval of constitutions has been experienced as often arbitrary, sometimes uninformed, and lacking in sensitivity to the particularly feminine embodiment of religious life emerging in the newly developed structures.[11] At this level all elements of collegiality appear often to be lost in a call for a kind of submission which reflects the worst elements of the clerical and patriarchal system. Ought not a woman to question whether she should spend her life engaging in such a system? Do not members come to religious life to live out the charism of their congregations within the family of the church, rather than to live out a univocal charism of religious life controlled by the authority of the ecclesial institution? Women, both potential candidates and seasoned religious, have difficulty here.

A similar difficulty centers around the handling of the signers of the *New York Times* ad. It is not the details of the case that are of interest here, but the way in which church authorities handled it. The action involved judgment without inquiry. Indeed it was immediate, arbitrary, and heavily authoritarian. Again, what is perceived and experienced is the worst aspects of clericalism and patriarchalism. Ought not a woman to question whether she should entrust her life to a system whose workings are marked not by a mutual respect and trust, but by the heavy-handed exercise of power? Do not members come to religious life to serve one another as disciples of Jesus, out of love for him present in his body the church? Women suffer painfully when that very body turns against them in an arbitrary way, without respect for them and their congregations.

The papal intervention in American apostolic religious life discussed in chapter 1 at first engendered fear analogous to that experienced in the aftermath of the case just mentioned. The problem here again was the apparent lack of trust on the part of the institutional church for American women religious.

Through the instrumentality of the papal commission, that situation developed into a supportive and encouraging dialogue. Whether it was perceived as such or not by potential candidates remains a question. Women religious are in a time of transition. For fifteen to twenty years sisters have been engaged in wholehearted efforts of renewal. What is needed is time to complete the process and then to appropriate its effects. During this period the structures of the church can best assist by offering support, questioning, and encouragement. The pontifical commission structured an intradiocesan and intraparish process that could enable the education of laity, priests, and bishops. It is to be hoped that the dialogue developed new support for the consideration of religious vocation on the part of women and support of that vocation by family, friends, and interested clergy.

Then there is the matter of the internal situation of women's religious congregations. When the potential candidate considers the congregations, what does she see? As one young woman stated, "If the members do not look convincing and convinced, forget it." Here there is a double problem. On the one hand, the problems connected with what I have called "the institutional face of the church" have, in some cases, engendered a climate in which it is very difficult to invite another woman in and to be properly welcoming to potential members. Families do not welcome guests during times of internal crisis, nor do they feel at ease welcoming the prospective spouses of their members at such times. So, too, it has been difficult for many religious women to encourage candidates when they themselves feel somewhat "under siege." Likewise, the very tenuousness of a time of transition does not create a good climate for the induction of new members. On the other hand, a second problem is connected directly with the declining numbers. There is an element here of self-fulfilling prophecy. The religious who dwells on the fewer numbers invites few in and so her congregation has yet fewer numbers. Both the problems connected with the institutional face of the church and the transition stage of religious congregations, along with the problems connected with shrinking numbers, affect morale and the ability of group members to generate new membership. The Spirit has always worked through the internalized living out of the charism of the group, a living out characterized by joy, to draw new members to congregations. Where that is not present, it is not surprising that new members do not come.[12]

Yet there are other questions religious women must ask when considering declining numbers. Are they counter-cultural enough? Are they *perceived* as giving of themselves? Is their identity evident to the average Catholic today? What of the struggle to live simply that others may simply live, while at the same time operating at levels of professional excellence to serve in the apostolate? This type of identity needs to be communicated. The amount of salary given to the common fund, the embracing of simple living in the face of materialism and even opulence, the willing dedication to celibate loving in the face of a sexually permissive culture, the discipline of self-will in the face of a me-first culture: these struggles to live the gospel need to be communicated. Sisters need, too, to communicate the nature of their faith commit-ment, that deepest and most intimate part of their lives. While their professionalism is apparent, how is their motiva-tion communicated? Many religious women are quite protec-tive about that. They need, finally, to communicate their new-found sense of the community that exists in the midst of diverse lifestyles. Sisters are learning to nurture the bond that unites them in many ways other than common roof and table.[13] Such factors need to be made apparent. One mother comments: "Unless you have a strong sense of community, what is there that my daughter can find among you that she cannot find as a single lay worker in the church?" Here the continuation of the dialogue process initiated by the pontifical commission is critical. Religious women have dialogued at length with one another about their changing understanding of religious life. They need to invite clergy and laity into the conversation, both to communicate what religious have learned, and to learn from clergy and laity as religious strug-gle with the problems that are still with them. Not the least of these problems are those that are due to the uneven pace at which members assimilate renewal and their disagreements about its direction. Yet honest and open dialogue about the situation is a vital step in the nurturing of new vocations. With so few sisters in the schools it is necessary to turn to new sources for contacts. An informed laity and clergy constitute a first step. A second step involves learning how to draw from those among whom and with whom religious women now work. This requires the sensitivity and patience to spend the time to nurture adult vocations which has been spent nurturing adolescent vocations.

FACTORS CONCERNING POTENTIAL CANDIDATES

There are a number of factors concerning potential candidates to take into account in considering the low entry rate. I referred to the nurturing of adult vocations, not adolescent vocations. One observation of those who are engaged in formation work is that the psychological maturing process is slow. That phenomenon is not restricted to persons presently in the formation process. The lengthy time spent in education, with the correlative delay of entry into adult life projects, has implications for readiness to make life choices. The situation is not simply that religious are no longer in schools in large numbers; it is also that students in schools are less ready to make life-choices. Their interest in religion is high, but it seems to be paired with low interest in institutional forms of religious commitment.

Another factor that needs reflection is why the poor—and particularly ethnic groups—have had difficulty both entering and remaining in congregations. Here religious need to examine their own prejudices as well as the cultures of the ethnic groups that form an increasingly large segment of American Catholics.

With the older and more mature candidate, there is the question of how to incorporate members already established in careers. With the younger candidate it is important to recognize the problem for a young person entering an older group. The situation may ask the woman of twenty-five or twenty-six to accept responsibility for a future with women whose median age is between fifty-five and sixty-five. To do this without a strong peer group may be extremely difficult. The challenge to the congregation is to find ways and means to permit peer bonding.

Thus, lack of readiness to make a life-choice, lack of ability to attract and to retain the poor and ethnics, uncertainty about how to incorporate mature applicants, and the burdens assumed by the few young in a predominantly older group are all factors affecting recruitment rate. There are steps that can be taken to redress a number of these difficulties. Whether doing so will prove to be the long-term remedy is another question.

A KEY EMPHASIS OF RELIGIOUS LIFE

Women come to religious life not for the vows but to live the gospel according to the charism of a specific community. Yet it remains true that to formalize the commitment to religious life women make public profession of the evangelical counsels by public vows. Those vows, and in particular the vow of celibacy, are absolutely distinctive of religious life. As Sandra Schneiders has remarked, this "is the only vow whose content has been a constant factor in all forms of religious life throughout history," and this remains the case although there have been various interpretations of the meaning of the vow.[14] I would go so far as to name consecrated celibacy an ultimate, irreducible aspect of the charism of religious life. To pledge celibacy for the kingdom is at the heart of religious life.[15]

It would not be surprising if this insight were to come to the fore in this sexually preoccupied culture. Poverty marked the new age of religious life in the thirteenth century, a century of burgeoning wealth. A high regard for poverty marked the mendicant orders which were established at that time. Obedience characterized the new dawn of religious life in the late sixteenth and early seventeenth centuries. That time was coincident with the rise of individualism in its various manifestations. The Jesuits are an example of an order that values obedience highly. Sexuality is a dominant concern of much of present-day society. The gift that witnesses to the transcendence of the gospel in the face of this preoccupation is consecrated celibacy. It especially characterizes the witness of religious in American society.

How does this vow relate to the question of declining numbers of religious in the changed and changing situation of the church in the United States? I respond with another question. Does the prospective candidate enter in order to maintain a particular form of life, or to engage in witness with her sisters? The religious life does not exist for the apostolate and ought not be identified with or reduced to its works. As it becomes clearer that there are not the numbers of religious required to maintain given works, it also becomes clearer that works are not (and never were) *the* key factor which identifies the religious. John Paul II recalls a longstanding tradition when he strongly situates religious vocation within the Christian vocation. He develops his understanding within the context of response to the questions of "why be a human person" and "how." He remarks that religious vocation involves learning who one is in the act of a particular way of following Jesus.[16]

The way religious follow Jesus is as witnesses to the gospel through a form of life marked by the public profession of the evangelical counsels, and most particularly through the public profession of celibacy for the sake of the kingdom. The life of consecrated celibacy will be filtered through the charism of the particular congregation, and so lived in varying circumstances, but it is recognizably a similar witness to the gospel in all the congregations. Following the Dominican tradition, Thomas Aquinas places the three vows as central and as principles. The ways in which one "disposes oneself to the observance of each" vary, and so orders vary from one another.[17] He finds room for works as widely varied as soldiering (he lived during the heyday of the military orders), business administration, and manual labor. His point is that anything can be done that helps our neighbor and serves God. It is the intention that matters.[18]

Religious today apply a similar principle in the attempt to relate the goals of foundresses and founders to changed circumstances. The combination of changed circumstances with declining numbers has led to dropped works. Dropped works are not in themselves a sign of the decline of religious life. Thomas affirms that "the religious state is directed to the attainment of the perfection of charity, consisting principally in the love of God and secondarily in the love of neighbor. Consequently *that which religious intend chiefly and for its own sake is to give themselves to God.* Yet if their neighbor be in need, they should attend to his affairs out of charity. . . ."[19] With his usual clarity Thomas subordinates works to the primary end of the life. That end consistently remains the gift of self which constitutes a particular witness to the gospel. A key element of that witness is consecrated celibacy.

Today in the United States that witness is vitally needed. Celibacy, however, is not the path for many but for few. The very nature of the kind of witness that is needed stipulates a small number. When religious live a life renewed in the spirit of their foundresses and founders and of the gospel, the candidates the Lord sends will come. They will come in order to share in the spirit of the congregation, and to do this they will embrace the vowed life, including celibacy. I believe that they will come in small numbers. The challenge is for religious to enable the laity to assume their rightful role in the church and to be content with smaller numbers. A reduction in numbers does not in itself constitute a crisis of vocations but can simply be God's unique gift to the American church now. The journey of religious today is a pilgrimage, one made with their sisters and brothers, lay and cleric. Their role on the pilgrimage is to witness to the kingdom through lives enspirited by the charisms of their congregations and consecrated to God through the witness of celibacy.

6
Leadership,
A Mutual Responsibility

Among ecclesial women the call of religious women is to radical totality of love within a community, and according to the charism of the community. The love is for Christ, expressed through love for others, namely, first for fellow religious within the community, and then for those whom they serve and all who, in one way or another, are their associates. Love is characteristic and it is basic. However, "love is a many splendored thing," and charism has to do with the particular splendor with which a given congregation glows. By charism I mean the gift of the Spirit for following Christ in and for the sake of the church. It involves a lifestyle including celibacy and a particular way of living community life, ecclesial ministry, and spirituality.[1] In a sense the gift of the charism of a particular community *is* the vocation. Each sister is pledged to live the gospel through her baptismal commitment according to the charism of the community through her religious profession. Religious entered for the sake of the love relationship, neither for the vows nor for the structures of religious life. All these structures, including those by which authority and accountability are exercised, are in service to the purpose of the community; that is, they exist to facilitate the charism of the community.

Community living today involves the appropriate exercise of authority and accountability in the mutual exercise of religious leadership. Leadership and governance are not coextensive terms. All are called to leadership; some—not always the ones who have best developed their leadership skills—are called to govern. Those who perform the service of governance exercise what Paul identified as the talent or gift for administration. At whatever level they work—local leader, regional or provincial superior, congregational president—the function of these women is to see to the smooth operation of the group. In this sense they are administrators like any other: the principal of the parish school, the mayor of a city, or the head of a business corporation. But these women are *religious* administrators. Beyond the smooth running of the group, their role includes challenging the group to fidelity to its charism. This is where their administration can and should become the exercise of religious leadership.

Administrators of a religious community, at all levels, are stewards of the charism. Nonetheless the charism belongs to all members, and all share in the responsibility for the appropriate exercise of authority and accountability. While this has been generally true for religious life in all its variations, the way it functions has varied considerably. The underlying principles affecting authority and accountability are already apparent in one of the great ancient rules, that of St. Augustine. It sheds light on the contemporary understanding of leadership as a mutual responsibility.

PATTERN FOR LEADERSHIP

The Rule of Saint Augustine,[2] dating from the end of the fourth century, is one of the four ancient rules[3] used in the church. Rules give patterns of life that have since been appropriated by numerous foundresses and founders, imbued with their own charisms, and ultimately used as the substructure of their constitutions. Since the eleventh century Augustine's rule has been widely used in this way. It is the rule, for example, that is foundational for the work of Vincent de Paul and of Elizabeth Seton, the foundress of the Sisters of Charity.

This rule supported a specific pattern of life in which authority and accountability were exercised in a specific way. The key to interpreting the document is that it was originally written for a group of friends who chose to live as *servi Dei* under Augustine's leadership. The rule consists of eight chapters covering fourteen pages in Van Bavel's edition. The second article in the first chapter states the foundational pattern of life for those who follow this rule. The basic ideal is mutual love. "Before all else, live together in harmony (Ps. 67 [68]:7), being of one mind and one heart (Acts 4:32) on the way to God."

Two stipulations are especially noteworthy. The first is the phrase "one mind and heart," which demands a certain amount of consensus. There must be agreement about ideals and goals if there is to be any concord. Some arrangements governing the common aspects of life will have to be accepted as normative "so long as the group recognizes itself" in these arrangements.[4] What is key is the recognition: "this is us." For example, it was typical of the Sisters of Charity of Cincinnati never to accept a true provincial structure even when the group was of considerable size. Movement between provinces was always fluid, and—most telling of all—finances remained centralized. The congregation had a strong sense of being one group and resisted anything destructive of its sense of unity. Ultimately, what a group identifies as itself is rooted in its charism that a rule does not embody but which various foundresses who use a rule specify for the group.

The pertinent phrase in Augustine's rule is not limited to "one mind and heart." "On the way to God" qualifies the phrase. Religious are together on the way to God. For genuine community life common table and common roof are not nearly as important as sharing in one another's life of faith. It is the inner life of ideas, hopes, expectations, fears, dreams, and the faith that supports them that is most valuable and which women religious are often most reluctant to share. This is what Augustine means when he states in a sermon: "You live together in the true sense of the word only if you have but one heart."[5] It is also probably true that a community that shares at the faith level is eagerly sought by those considering religious life today.

From this step the rule moves immediately to article three:

the sharing of material goods. Such sharing belongs to the very first stage of love. Lovers give of what they have to those they love. In community a consequence of this exercise is the elimination of distinctions, which—in Augustine's day as well as in ours—is a countercultural stance. The rest of the chapter spells out its meaning, that is, radical gospel equality which in the late fourth century was thought of as between free and slave, rich and poor. Today it is between black, Hispanic, white, Oriental, Indian; between rich and poor; between women and men. This equality is continually countercultural, and so socially critical.

The challenge is to live an ideal calling for mutual love expressed in unity of mind and heart on the way to God and enfleshed in a community of goods. A review of the chapter subjects for the rest of the rule identifies the intent. The subjects include: chapter 2, prayer; chapter 3, community and care of the body; chapter 4, mutual responsibility in good and evil; chapter 5, service of one another; chapter 6, love and conflict; and chapter 7, love in authority and obedience, followed by chapter 8, an exhortation. Four chapters (4, 5, 6, 7) address religious leadership in the sense of appropriate exercise of authority and accountability.

But who appropriately exercises leadership? None of the four chapters is addressed to officeholders. In fact each of these chapters is concerned with the entire community.

Chapter 4 handles common responsibility for one another's faults and how to exercise it. If religious are about going to God together, it is a legitimate concern to ask about their direction. Religious have a responsibility to help one another along the way. In more modern terms, this chapter of the rule is saying that if one should see a sister who is drinking too much, or is never at community meetings, or is giving scandal by a love relationship, members of her community have a responsibility for her. Members might reflect on when they last, out of love, spoke to someone about such a situation or considered how to handle it. Or, they might reflect on when and how they have dealt with such a situation as a local group. This rule calls for that and bases its authority on the gospel.

Sisters have responsibility for one another and are accountable to one another. Matthew and Paul (1 Tim. 5:20) empha-
size this quality. The Matthean passage exhorts:

> If your sister sins against you, go and tell her her fault,
> between you and her alone. If she listens to you, you have
> gained your sister. But if she does not listen, take one or two
> others along with you, that every word may be confirmed by
> the evidence of two or three witnesses. If she refuses to listen
> to them, tell it to the church; and if she refuses to listen even
> to the church, let her be to you as a Gentile and a tax collector.

In applying this mandate, the rule adds the following paragraph:

> Imagine, for example, that your sister had a physical wound
> which she wanted to conceal for fear of undergoing medical
> treatment. Would it not be heartless of us to say nothing about
> it? Rather, would it not be an act of mercy on our part to make
> it known? How much greater, then, is our obligation to make
> our sister's condition known and to prevent evil gaining a
> stronger hold in her heart, something much worse than a
> physical wound.[6]

Throughout, the stress is on the love that lies behind and
permeates the entire episode.

Chapter 4 does assign a role to the group leader. Her task,
once the situation is resolved sister to sister, is to decide "what
punishment should be meted out." Religious today would also
expect leadership to take firm action in the extreme case of
public scandal, e.g., the case of a religious publicly involved
in a sexual liaison.

Chapter 5 specifies caring for one another's needs. The
congregation is to provide for food, clothing, hygiene, books.
Most important is the inner motivation. If all receive from the
common purse according to need, then no one will seek her
own advantage in her work. All that is done will be for the
service of the community, so

the degree to which you are concerned for the interests of the community rather than for your own, is the criterion by which you can judge how much progress you have made. Thus in all the fleeting necessities of human life something sublime and permanent reveals itself, namely love. (Cf. 1 Cor. 12:31—"I will show you a yet more excellent way"; 13:13—"So faith, hope and love abide, these three, but the greatest of these is love.")[7]

Sisters' care for the group is an expression of their love.

Each is to use the authority entrusted her by the group to care for the needs of the group. Each is accountable to the community for this exercise of authority delegated by the community and each is accountable to her own conscience.

Chapter 4 addressed the problem of failure to live up to the community ideal while chapter 5 dealt with care for external needs. Chapter 6 treats one of the most sensitive areas in religious life. One might call it the great internal need, and once more it is for charity. How do sisters handle disagreement, or quarrels? The entire chapter operates on the following principle:

Sisters who have insulted each other should forgive each other's trespasses (Matt. 6:12); if you fail to do this, your praying the Our Father becomes a lie. Indeed, the more you pray, the more honest your prayer ought to become.[8]

Each is responsible for her own relationships directly to the Lord and indirectly through those with whom she relates. The need is love supported by "honest prayer," or at least prayer trying to grow in honesty.

Chapter 7 follows with its section on love in authority and obedience. Love holds a prominent place. Whether one exercises authority or responds to it in obeying, the emphasis is on love. In essence the rule describes the duties of the leader as service in love, guidance, and example, while obedience is viewed as an act of compassionate love. The leader is to be concerned for living out the community ideal. She is to call others to account when they lapse. She is herself to model living that ideal (Titus 2:7). She is "to reprimand those who neglect their work, to give courage to those who are disheartened, to support the weak, and to be patient with everyone" (1 Thess. 5:14).

None of these services, however, is a task assigned to her alone. All share in these responsibilities. The list is worth rereading: "Reprimand those who neglect their work, give courage to those who are disheartened, support the weak, be patient with everyone." The rule quotes 1 Thessalonians addressed to all Christians. In brief, the gospel exhortation is respected by the rule which expects all members to exercise their Christian responsibility, assuming their appropriate authority for one another, and being accountable to one another. Mutual correction remains critically important, while the leader is assigned a final role in reconciliation (chapter 4).

Likewise, it is the general superior who speaks for the group. For Augustine, as Von Bavel notes, "responsibility is not concentrated in one person, but is spread over the entire group."[9] This is extraordinary considering the social structures of Augustine's day. He does not accept the established structures. He offers an alternate form of society.

In the second half of chapter 7, obedience as compassion is based on Augustine's understanding of how humans experience themselves in spiritual poverty. Only God can alleviate it—so to love God is the greatest service human beings can do for themselves. To live uprightly and in goodness out of love is the first charity humans perform for themselves. To care for their own well-being in this deepest sense is to love themselves truly; not to do so is to bring death on themselves. To listen to one another, and to obey the superior, is for Augustine primarily an act of this kind of love.

It is furthermore an act of mercy to the superior. Since the office is a burden, to obey is to lighten the burden of another. As Van Bavel expresses it: "The other members of the community allow the burden borne by the one responsible for the group to weigh on them as well; they too bear this burden; together they put their shoulders to the task."[10] Finally, the one in office is in a dangerous situation. The exercise of leadership in office is subject to all the dangers associated with the use of power. Responsible obedience joined to the responsible exercise of leadership at all levels of religious life will decrease the danger and activate compassion for the sister in office, decreasing in her any tendency to abuse power.[11]

In summary, the *Rule of St. Augustine* presents religious leadership, understood as the appropriate exercise of authority and accountability, as diffused throughout the community with appropriate functions being assigned to the superior. There are evident applications for today going even beyond those already adduced.

COLLEGIALITY AND SUBSIDIARITY

What is called for in the principles of renewal established by Vatican II is the application in a new form of the spirit of Augustine's rule, a rule developed for a community of friends bound by love. In the area of leadership, this is achieved by applying the principles of collegiality and subsidiarity in the exercise of authority and accountability.

By collegiality I mean the recognition that religious are members of a community and function as sisters who share a collective authority or responsibility for the community, and are accountable to the community. By subsidiarity I mean that the decision rests at the level closest to the implementation of the decision. Leadership is the voice that calls to responsibility and accountability. In a typical set of constitutions, these principles are delineated thus:

> Religious authority resides in all our superiors by reason of their office and in the General Chapter when in session. Each of us has a certain authority which is exercised responsibly within the framework of our commitment as Sisters of Charity. We participate in decision-making by incorporating the principles of subsidiarity, collegiality, and accountability into the various phases of Congregational life.[12]

This is a twentieth- and twenty-first–century expression of principles first articulated in the *Rule of St. Augustine,* rules to shape life among a community of friends.

Such principles involve a number of implications for daily living. I will use three examples of decision dialogues. In no. 1 the first voice is that of the sister; in no. 2 the first voice belongs to the local community; while in no. 3 the first voice is that of the general leadership.

Example no. 1 concerns an individual's placement in ministry. Here a sister recognizes a job she believes fits her gifts and the charism of the community. Her voice expresses this to the community. She exercises leadership here. It is her gifts and her life that are coming to expression in a given job, yet she does not lead or choose alone. She is a member of the community. In carrying out her job she will stand as a public witness, living the charism of the community. The exercise of leadership around ministerial placement is dialogical or collegial. As the sister's voice speaks as an individual member, so those the group has chosen as leaders or special custodians of the charism speak to verify the decision the member is making. That verification will be an exercise in discernment. The elected leaders will challenge, clarify, affirm the correspondence between the sister's proposed work and the charism of the community.

In this example the individual sister's voice initiated the discernment dialogue brought to conclusion in a communal or collegial context. Many examples are possible but the principles remain the same: the individual exercises responsibility for what affects her life directly (subsidiarity), but does so as a member of the community and so in dialogue with the leadership of those the group has trusted to guard the charism (collegiality). Details vary from one congregation to another, but the principles of collegiality and subsidiarity remain constant. Accountability in this case is to the general leadership because it is through her ministry that the sister acts publicly to incarnate the charism of the community.

The second example involves a decision to be made by a

local community about any of numerous concerns, including a budget, social justice, a way of opening the faith-life of the group to laity. In the latter situation several sisters in the local house value an invitation to interested laity to share a meal, discussion, and prayer around mutual growth in gospel living on a monthly basis. Other members of the house oppose this as interference with their privacy and inappropriate mixing with laity. There are several possible outcomes: drop the project; the naysayers drop opposition to the project; the house explores the causes for their divisions, comes to better mutual understanding, and develops another, mutually satisfactory project on similar lines; the house splits.

What is of concern here is the process by which decision is reached. Leadership is being exercised within the group in the voicing of a possible way to live the gospel through the charism. The first step is to explore possibilities together. (The assumption is that the suggestion was not irresponsible but contains some real possibilities.) The second step is to examine the possibilities in light of the responsibilities of the group for and to one another to live the gospel in the form shaped by the charism of their congregation. The third step is to decide, and the fourth step is to inform general (or regional) leadership of a local decision. Why? Accountability in this case is to one another in the local group and to the rest of the community through those elected to guard the charism. Again, general or regional leadership may act to affirm, to challenge, to clarify the decision.

In the third example the general leadership takes initiative about any area related to corporate life. Examples include: building a retirement facility for the sisters; buying into someone else's retirement facility; building a health-care facility, or buying into a health-care program. The initiative in such a project appropriately comes from the general leadership. They explain the need, pose the options, make clear the availability of funds. Such a major investment affecting the entire congregation appropriately requires input from the congregation and accountability to the congregation. Why?

The congregation stewards the charism together. All are members. The common goods belong to all, and the responsibility for one another is a mutual responsibility.

CONCLUSION

Three implications arise from these reflections on leadership and the decision-making style:

(1) Religious have a responsibility to know and to internalize the charism of the congregation. It is the first principle of discernment and a basic responsibility of every member. It is key to the personal exercise of religious leadership and a dominant factor in the experience of religious leadership.

(2) Leadership begins with the internalizing of conscience and the appropriation of one's own legitimate sense of authority. Whose choice was it to enter? To stay? To work as hard as each one does in ministry? Conscience is at work here. It needs to work as well in broader areas of responsibility for and toward the community. But never ought conscience function in a splendid vacuum. Rather conscience for a religious is informed by the charism and operates in a dialogue of discernment with sisters and with group leadership.

(3) Structures of governance are necessary to enable leadership to function. Congregations consistently seek the shifts in the structure of governance that will best reflect a spirituality like that of the Augustinian rule so that a congregation will become (a) a community shaped by gospel equality; (b) a community motivated by love; (c) and a community socially critical.

In the life of American women religious today witness is offered through a life of consecrated celibacy lived in a community marked by leadership accepted as a mutual responsibility and so characterized in the post–Vatican II era by collegiality and accountability.

7

Catherine,
A Preeminent Ecclesial Woman

What does it mean to be a woman of the church? We have seen women express that identity in the struggle to shape diverse forms of religious life and through the witness of a variety of lay ministries. We have addressed the question of women's status in the church. We have reflected on the implications of smaller numbers of religious women, the relationship of that fact to a lifestyle of consecrated celibacy. We have considered the experience of community marked by the experience of leadership accepted as a mutual responsibility. Throughout it has been apparent that women religious are laywomen who seek to live out the baptismal commitment that unites them to Christ through the church by a particular form of life. Their lay status is a bond uniting them to all women of the church as is the experience of sexism, a problem common to all women.

Let us consider now one woman's answer to the question "What does it mean to be an ecclesial woman?" Catherine of Siena, a fourteenth-century laywoman, author, and doctor of the church,[1] contributes an understanding of what it is to be an ecclesial person. I will use "woman" and "women" as inclusive terms here, recognizing that Catherine is referring to all people. It will be evident that the lessons learned from Catherine's teaching can be readily applied to women's common experience of sexism today.

THE GOSPEL ACCORDING TO CATHERINE

It is in the *Dialogue* that Catherine presents her understanding of discipleship.[2] She makes clear what it is to believe,
that is, to enter into a relationship with Jesus and to be sent on
mission. Two basic assumptions govern Catherine as an ecclesial woman which she explains in the first two chapters of the
Dialogue, developing them in chapters 3 through 12. Her first
assumption is the intimate interconnection between truth and
love. In her opening chapter Catherine speaks of a woman full
of love who wants to act out of love to bring glory to God and
God to all:

> A soul rises up, restless with tremendous desire for God's
> honor and the salvation of souls. She . . . has become ac-
> customed to dwelling in the cell of self-knowledge in order to
> know better God's goodness toward her since upon knowledge
> follows *love*. (*Dial*. 1)

How did that woman become full of love? Catherine says she
dwelt in the cell of self-knowledge. In truly knowing themselves human beings at one and the same time find humility
and come to know God. This is because when they know the
truth about themselves they see that even their own existence
comes from God. In the *Dialogue* God says:

> You will find humility in the knowledge of yourself when you
> see that even your own existence comes not from yourself but
> from me, for I loved you before you came into being. And in
> my unspeakable love for you I willed to create you anew in
> grace. So I washed you and made you a new creation in the
> blood that my only-begotten Son poured out with such burn-
> ing love. (*Dial*. 4; see also 9–12)

Humility, self-knowledge, and knowledge of God are thus
conjoined. This leads to charity for the following reasons.
When people know the truth about themselves false self-love
is rejected. Those who know what their fears are, what their
hungers are, who are in touch with the depth of their own

vulnerability are not likely to have a mistaken love for themselves. This frees them for genuine love. And all genuine love is the touch of God who is love. Catherine would say that once humans are free from selfish love they are in touch with the truth (who is God), and so catch fire with "unspeakable love" (*Dial.* 4). The first assumption governing Catherine as an ecclesial woman is the intimate link between truth and love. In establishing this link she describes the basic pattern of life for the disciple. While this assumption is the common teaching of the church, it is still particularly appropriate to Catherine as an ecclesial woman and an ecclesial woman in the Dominican tradition. *Veritas,* truth, and *caritas,* love, are the motto of the Dominican Order. The *Dialogue* begins:

> A soul rises up, restless with tremendous desire for God's honor and the salvation of souls. She has for some time exercised herself in virtue and has become accustomed to dwelling in the cell of self-knowledge in order to know better God's goodness toward her, since upon knowledge follows love. And loving, she seeks to pursue truth and clothe herself in it. (*Dial.* 1)

There is also a second assumption here. God reminds Catherine that "the reasoning creature" has a beauty and dignity that come from being created in God's image and likeness, a beauty further enhanced by charity. Such human beings are united to God in love, and in a touching phrase God is made to say "they are another me" (*Dial.* 1). With this basic assumption Catherine lays the groundwork for her presentation of the doctrine of John 14:21–23: "If you love me and keep my word, I will show myself to you, and you will be one thing with me and I with you"; and of Matthew 25:40b: "As you did it to one of the least of these my sisters, you did it to me."

Basically this means that God is present to the lovers of God, but the test of love for God is love for one another. The sisters and brothers whom Christ points out in Matthew's Gospel deserve their sisters' love. To withhold that love, and in particular to refrain from the good that could be done them,

is to do harm. Catherine's thought may be paraphrased somewhat like this: "When I think I don't have time for *her* because
she is less educated, *she* is not sympathetic with my lifestyle,
or *he* irritates me, or *they* are street people and they frighten
me—when these reasons are rooted in lack of love and therefore I withhold the good I might do, this is sin, just as
positively vicious acts are sinful" (*Dial.* 6). The reasoning
creature has a beauty and dignity that come from being created in God's image and likeness, and consequently what is
done to one another is done to God.

An ecclesial woman following Catherine, then, is one for
whom love and truth are deeply interrelated. In Dominican
spirituality self-knowledge leads to knowledge of God, which
grounds love. The test for divine love is love of neighbor. The
rational creature is the image and likeness of God and an
ecclesial woman expresses her love for God in her treatment of
her sisters and brothers. So the concept of mission is con-
tained within the understanding of the ecclesial woman, not
only within the gospel picture but also in Catherine's presentation of this picture.

THE MISSION OF THE ECCLESIAL WOMAN

Catherine's description of the one in love with God's truth is
striking:

> Blessed with this unitive love she reaches out in loving charity
> to the whole world's need for salvation. But beyond a general
> love for all people she sets her eye on the specific needs of her
> neighbors and comes to the aid of those nearest her according
> to the graces I have given her for ministry. (*Dial.* 7)

It is important here to notice both the focus of concern and the
implementation of the focus in action. There is an interplay
set up between the whole world and the immediate neighbor.

This is further clarified by the petitions Catherine offers in
the next major section of the *Dialogue* (chaps. 13 through 25).

First she prays for mercy for the people of God and the church (*Dial*. 13–15), then for mercy for the world (*Dial*. 16–19), and finally for grace to follow the way of truth for a most immediate neighbor (*Dial*. 20–25). As a top priority in her prayer the ecclesial woman holds the needs of the church. In his book on ministry, Richard McBrien develops her thought:

> Ministers and candidates for ministry at whatever level cannot be fundamentally in doubt about the necessity and purpose of the Church. All ministry is in service of the Church. It has no other purpose than to serve the People of God and to advance the mission they have received from Christ. Ministers and ministerial candidates [all the more, I would insist, ecclesial women] must also have a practical understanding of and commitment to the gospel consistent with ecclesial faith, or faith in the Church.[3]

Such faith in the church is compatible with loving criticism, but it must precede and sustain that criticism. The ecclesial woman loves the church, is aware of its defects, and keeps its needs as her top priority. It is well known that Catherine was passionately concerned about the sinfulness of clerics and of the pope. This knowledge did not lead her to disaffection with the church but rather to effective involvement in reform of the church. In her model such involvement begins in prayer, and change is rooted in God's response to that loving prayer. It is important to note that involvement does not end with prayer, but it must *begin* and find its sustenance there.

Catherine's next petition is for God's mercy on the whole world. The loving concern of the ecclesial woman is not limited to the church, but it extends to the needs of all those whom the woman from Siena would call "God's rational creatures." In response to this petition God showed her the whole world within the divine hand and said:

> They are mine; I created them, and I love them ineffably. And so, in spite of their wickedness, I will be merciful to them because of my servants, and I will grant what you have asked of me with such love and sorrow. (*Dial*. 18)

The point for ecclesial women is that God's mercy to the world is made dependent on the loving intercession of God's servants. Again, the responsibility to pray, to hold the world in their praying hearts.

But Americans typically want to move quickly from prayer to action. Some outlines of that path to action for an ecclesial woman are indicated in Catherine's third petition, her prayer that her beloved Raymond of Capua follow the way of truth. The way of truth is Christ, the bridge to heaven. It is necessary to stay on the bridge while carrying out one's responsibilities as a worker in the vineyard of the church (*Dial*. 24). Catherine's metaphors are a bit mixed here, but her point is fairly clear. She is praying that her beloved friend follow the way of truth, follow Christ in carrying out his responsibilities as a minister in the church.

When God describes to Catherine the role of the churchly minister, there are distinctions worth noting. The call to the vineyard is founded in baptism. The administration of the sacraments is reserved to the ordained. However, all the baptized are to work both in the vineyard of their own souls and in the universal body of Christianity. Addressing all the baptized, God says "You then are my workers. You have come from me, the supreme eternal gardener, and I have engrafted you onto the vine by making myself one with you" (*Dial*. 24). While each one is to work in her plot, her neighbors' plots are not separated by any dividing lines. Whatever good or evil they do for themselves affect their neighbors. Thus God says to Catherine:

> All of you together make up one common vineyard, the whole Christian assembly, and you are all united in the vineyard of the mystic body of holy Church from which you draw your life. In the vineyard is planted the vine, which is my only-begotten Son, into whom you must be engrafted. Unless you are engrafted into him you are rebels against holy Church, like members that are cut off from the body and rot. (*Dial*. 24)

What is spelled out here is the application to mission of the gospel assumptions governing the notion of the ecclesial woman. The prayer Catherine makes for Raymond each ecclesial woman might make for herself and one another: that they might follow Christ, the way of life, that they might be united to Christ, the living vine, in all of their ministry, particularly in that ministry which most immediately presents itself to them, the ministry to themselves and those closest to them, their neighbors, that is, their sisters and associates.

ECCLESIAL WOMEN FOR WOMEN

If women religious are to act on the implication of this prayer of Catherine today they will take seriously the needs and concerns of women. Sexism is a problem facing all women, whether in the church or in the larger society. It is increasingly recognized as a problem beyond the borders of this country. Witness the interventions favoring improving the place of women in the church made at the 1987 Roman synod by bishops from outside the United States. Within the church the scope of the problem is easily indicated: sexism touches language, reproductive ethics, decision-making, and office-holding.

The male bias in language, that is, the dominant use of *man* or *men* and the masculine pronoun when the intent is to speak of all humankind, serves to etch in consciousness the subordinate position of women. While this is a societal problem, it is reflected in the church with particular poignancy in that through it the language of the scriptures and ritual serves as a tool for the exclusion of women. Furthermore, the exclusive use of the male pronoun to denominate God introduces subliminally the heretical proposition that God is male. The explicit faith is that God is beyond gender; actual practice implicitly renders the image and concept of God as male. This is a disservice to both women and men.

Within the church sexism is apparent in the field of reproductive ethics. A large part of the difficulty hinges on the absence of women's experience. For too long women were excluded from scholarship, and they remain largely excluded from the decision-making arena. Thus women's voices remain unheard and sometimes have been positively excluded. For example, there appears to have been no consultation with married women in the discussion of procreative technology preceding the publication in 1987 of an instruction on that subject by the Congregation for the Doctrine of the Faith.[4] The discussion of this entire area of ethics is affected by the fact that as consciousness of sexism is raised, there is a slowly developing change in the relationship between women and men. Consideration of this change in the relationship should be conjoined to consideration of the technological developments in controlling reproduction. To exclude concern for the changing relationship from consideration of changes in reproductive technology is to maintain a sexist reproductive ethic.

I have already discussed, particularly in chapter 4, the exclusion of women from decision-making in the church. This is problematic on many levels, from the parish to the Vatican. While it is distinct from the exclusion of women from office, the two are related. Most decision-makers within the church are, in fact, ordained clerics. Since to exercise decision-making is consistent with the exercise of complete, adult human powers, to exclude one sex from the use of that power is to raise questions about whether one views that sex as fully human.

The exclusion of women from ordained ministry is a disciplinary decision depending in fact on psychological and sociological reasons. It is extraordinarily difficult if not impossible to justify this position theologically.[5]

There are thus four major arenas within the church in which sexism is felt: the use of exclusive language, the field of reproductive ethics, and exclusion from decision-making, as well as from ordained ministry. Within the larger North American society it may well be true that the major instance of sexism today is the feminization of poverty, linked to job and pay discrimination. The plight of a former Los Angeles TV anchor-woman illustrates the problem: rendered homeless through the loss of work, she was offered a job contingent upon her willingness to strip and stand nude before her would-be employer. The example speaks for itself.

It is true that for a growing minority women's experience is the experience of poverty. Two of every three poor adults in this country are women. A 1981 study concluded that if the current trend continues at the same rate, "the poverty population would be composed solely of women and their children before the year 2000."[6] Again, I discussed this in chapter 4.

At fault in all of this are the sexist structures of private economy, reinforced by federal, state, and city governments. Reflection on this current experience of women in the light of the gospel cries aloud for structural change. The human dignity of women and the requirements of justice demand this.

A PROBLEM OF PRACTICAL CONSCIENCE

If women religious today are to adopt Catherine's interpretation of what it is to be ecclesial women, informed by truth and love and serving the needs of those immediate to them, much is expected of them, not least in the area of women's needs. The situation of women requires that those concerned understand the issues, foster dialogue on them in church and society, confront injustices toward women, and take actions that lead to full participation of women from all cultures in both church and society. There is a twofold problem here. The first is that the ordinary obligations and responsibilities of life are already demanding and time-consuming. The second is a problem endemic to the human condition. That is, when coping with something challenging like sexism the human tendency is to see it as someone else's problem rather than as one's own. It is easiest to recognize and deal with it outside in the larger society or even in the church. It is extremely difficult to recognize and deal with it within one's own situa-

tion. It requires something of a true conversion to confess to
sexism and to eradicate it from one's own life and ministry.

This last step brings us back to Catherine's true self-knowledge. In her view humans are nothing, not even loving toward
one another, of themselves. The instances of a person's lack of
true love for her sisters are the measure of her self-centered-
ness. This is her sin. And it partakes of sexism when a woman
in a community of women cannot find love in her heart toward
a sister of sisters. To the measure that such love is present it is
the gift of the God who is love and who calls her and her
sisters into being in an act of boundless love. A touchstone for
the genuineness of love for God is a woman's treatment of her
sisters.

In the same way the touchstone of a congregation's love for
God is its treatment of its members. Words often cannot be
heard because of the clamor of actions. Do the actions of
religious toward one another as individuals and as a congregation bear witness to the reality and depth of their love for
one another? That is the opposite of sexism. Sexism turns
against the members of one sex and denies them their human
dignity; does the example of sisters in their treatment of
sisters show the opposite? What does their use of langauge
reveal? And how do their decision-making processes function
with respect to membership and mission? Finally, is the climate within the congregation such as to foster that genuine
love which fulfills the basic human need for intimacy and so
offers true celibate witness? Catherine begins always in mission with her immediate neighbor. Within community life the
immediate neighbor is the sister-religious. In the most vital
sense, charity begins at home.

Charity does not rest there. It moves out into personal
ministries, the places in which sisters serve on a daily basis.
Again sisters' use of language and decision-making style are
useful indicators. Do women use inclusive language in their
speech? In their God-talk? Is their decision-making inclusive
of those affected by their decisions? Is it supportive of the
needs of women? Attitudinal changes are required. Sisters

must become something other, learning to act from the center where Love lives. This is much more important than that they do something different.

Charity, however, does not rest there. Direct action is needed if there is to be change. Some must direct their energy in mission to bringing about the needed changes in church and society. Sensitivity to the gifts given for ministry is crucial. To return to Catherine's language, in the *Dialogue* God says:

> Beyond a general love for all people [the ecclesial woman] sets her eye on the specific needs of her neighbors and comes to the aid of those nearest her according to the graces I have given her for ministry. Some she teaches by word, giving sincere and impartial counsel; others she teaches by her example—as everyone ought to—edifying her neighbors by her good, holy, honorable life. (*Dial*. 7)

Some sisters are gifted for scholarship. Their tasks include: to redress the use of exclusive language, to help us relearn history and reformulate spirituality, to assist in developing a reproductive ethic inclusive of women's experience. Other sisters are gifted with leadership to begin the movement of women into decision-making roles. Still others have gifts to work against the feminization of poverty. There are many other gifts. Each one is called to examine the gift given her for ministry and to use it for the good of the church according to the mission of the congregation.

The problem in practical conscience is threefold. Each must reflect on the orientation of her own heart, as evidenced in her actions toward her sisters. The congregation is called to examine its orientation as apparent in its use of language and its treatment of members. Every sister in mission is accountable for her use of language and her style of decision-making; some sisters are called to exercise the gifts for ministry directly in tackling sexism-related issues.

It is perhaps not too fanciful to think that Catherine herself

might bless such an endeavor in the language of a thirteenth-
century Dominican blessing:

> May God the Father bless us, may God the Son heal us, may
> the Holy Spirit enlighten us and give us eyes to see with, ears
> to hear with, and hands to do the work of God with, feet to
> walk with, and a mouth to preach the word of salvation with,
> and the angel of peace to watch over us and lead us at last, by
> our Lord's gift, to the kingdom. Amen. [7]

8
Faith-filled Women

As ecclesial women move toward their future, bearing rich blessings in themselves and for others, it is essential that they be women of faith. To be faith-filled women means to be midwives, to be courageous, to be women for others. This is my vision of ecclesial women who are religious. It is a vision of courageous midwives, visibly assisting in the birth of life in all its richness. The articulation of this vision calls for a visionary technique for its expression. Thus what follows is less formal and more intimate in style. It relies on story and direct address to convey reflections of a more personal nature.

MIDWIVES AT THE BIRTH OF NEW LIFE

I begin with a biblical story. Once upon a time long ago and far away in Egypt there came to power a new king. "Look," he said to his subjects, "these people, the children of Israel, have become so numerous and strong that they threaten us. We must be prudent and take steps against their increasing any further, or if war should break out, they might add to the number of our enemies." The Egyptians forced the children of Israel into slavery and made their lives unbearable with hard labor, work with clay and brick, all kinds of work in the fields. They forced on them every kind of labor.

The king of Egypt then spoke to the Hebrew midwives. One of the midwives was named Shiphrah and the other Puah. (These are the only two in this story whose names are known.) The king said to them: "When you midwives attend

Hebrew women, watch carefully when they are about to give birth. If it is a boy, kill him; if a girl, let her live." But Shiphrah and Puah were God-fearing. They disobeyed the command of the king of Egypt and let the boys live. So the king of Egypt summoned the midwives. "Why," he asked them, "have you done this and spared the boys?" They answered: "The Hebrew women are not like Egyptian women. They are hardy, and they give birth quickly before the midwife reaches them." God was kind to the midwives. The people increased and grew very powerful. Since the midwives reverenced God, God granted the people descendants.

Shiphrah and Puah grasped the midwife's role: to bring life to birth. For the good of their country they were ordered to destroy life. They knew, even before the commandment was given to Moses, that in a choice between life and death God asks that humans choose life. They were faith-filled women. The choice before them was not simple. In choosing life for the boy babies, Shiphrah and Puah also chose the possibility of death for themselves.

What is happening in this story? At most it presents an early instance of passive resistance to earthly power on grounds of conscience. These midwives, assisting at the birth of life in the face of death-dealing oppression, are among the first recorded conscientious objectors. That is a maximum interpretation. What is the minimum interpretation? At least the story hints at a deeper meaning to life than the physical life of the babies. That meaning would not come to full expression until many centuries later. Then the Son of another Hebrew woman would teach: "Anyone who wants to save her life will lose it; but anyone who loses her life for my sake will find it" (Matt. 16:25). "Unless a grain of wheat falls on the ground and dies, it remains only a single grain; but if it dies, it yields a rich harvest. Anyone who loves her life loses it; anyone who hates her life in this world will keep it for the eternal life" (John 12:24–25).

Shiphrah and Puah act as midwives to new life in the face of oppression, trusting in God rather than in the king. If this story is a pattern for women's apostolic spirituality, one of its assumptions is that women know their God, listen to God, are learning to recognize the word that is of God. But to whom do women listen? How do they hear their God? How do they become faith-*filled*? This calls for another story, a story set in a home on a hot summer day. Three wayfarers—hot, tired, and thirsty—arrive on the doorstep. The big city American response might well be to call the police, or perhaps to direct the wanderers to the nearest travelers' aid. The small town does it differently.

So, too, does the Near East. Even today hospitality there requires ministering to the needs of guests. Remember Sarah, whose husband Abraham welcomed three such strangers? In return the guests promised that the elderly Sarah would bear a son. In the often robust words of Genesis, Sarah laughed at the unlikelihood of such pleasure coming her way again. The narrative continues: "Yahweh dealt kindly with Sarah as he had said, and did what he had promised her. So Sarah conceived and bore a son to Abraham in his old age, at the time God had promised. . . . Then Sarah said, 'God has given me cause to laugh; all those who hear of it will laugh with me'" (Gen. 21:1–7). Sarah's laughter comes first in surprise, and then when her child Isaac has been born she laughs for sheer joy. Her laughter in the story plays on Isaac's name, which means "God has smiled and been kind." Where did Sarah hear God? The words of the strangers are the first, the surprising instance of God's message to Sarah. The embrace of her husband, the changes in her own body, and the birth of the child are evidence of God's smile and kindness. To whom do women listen to hear God? It seems clear that they listen to strangers (especially surprising and unexpected ones), to their dear ones, to their own bodies.

This recalls the incident of a stranger in conversation with a woman whom he did not know was a sister. In the course of their talk she happened to mention her identity. The spontaneous response was, "But you're too happy to be a sister." There's plenty of food for thought there. It's wonderful if a sister's happiness is visible. Clearly this man's experience of sisters was not an experience of happy women. The entire vignette can feed prayer. Through the word of the unexpected stranger, God can speak.

But to whom else do we listen to hear God? Where do we meet God? Is this the whole story? There is another familiar account of a listening woman. Luke records: "In the sixth month the angel Gabriel was sent by God to a town in Galilee called Nazareth, to a virgin bethrothed to a man named Joseph, of the House of David; and the virgin's name was Mary. He went in and said to her, 'Rejoice, so highly favored!'" Where was Mary, and what was she doing? Our ideas are colored by centuries of religious art. The text does not say Mary was in her room. It is very unlikely she *had* a room of her own. No one knows where Mary was or what she was doing. What the text does record about Mary is her state of life, the thing that is significant for the story. She was betrothed but still a virgin. The whole encounter with Gabriel is shaped by that fact. This clear-sighted young woman receives what is presented as a direct message from God. Her first action is to weigh the message in the light of what her state in life asks of her. The story continues: "'Rejoice so highly favored! The Lord is with you.' She was deeply disturbed by these words and asked herself what this greeting could mean, but the angel said to her: 'Mary, do not be afraid; you have won God's favor. Listen! You are to conceive and bear a son, and you must name him Jesus'" (Luke 1:26–32). Then Mary asks how this can be since she is a virgin. Her state of life was shaped by previous solemn choices, evidently carefully made. Mary tested the message against her understanding of her obligations coming from these previous choices. Only when the compatibility of the two things was clear—her present virginity and commitment to Joseph on the one hand, and the angel's message on the other hand—did she recognize the message from God and give her consent.

For Mary the framework of her life had an important role in the mediation of God's presence. This model directs attention to the ones who shape that framework for apostolic religious women. Certainly these include sister religious and certainly superiors. While it is true that sisters can live and work at a distance from the congregation because the apostolate calls them there, a sister can *never* work *independently* of the congregation of which she is a member. Membership, and so fellow members, shape the framework of her life. Certainly, too, associates in the ministry and those who are served are among the mediators of God's presence. That presence is further mediated through a congregation's relationship to the great church, including the relationship to the bishops and the Holy See. Mother Seton's dying injunction to the early American community reflects the heritage of American women religious: "Be daughters of the church." God seeks to be present, filling these women in and through all their ecclesial life, and in and through all their congregational ministries—whether they are serving with Hispanics and blacks, or teaching grade six; whether they are hospital administrators, or struggling for nuclear disarmament; whether they are lonely researchers, or nurses, or far-flung missioners. My point here is not to itemize every possible individual work; rather, it is to recall that these diverse works are carried out as ministries *in* the church. Every congregation is *in* the church; the church is the place in which God will fill religious women so that as faith-filled women they can be midwives to new life.

In the first part of this chapter we have seen that the faith-filled woman is a midwife, helping bring to birth life in all its richness. To do that she must permit the God who is life to fill her. We have also reflected on where she meets that God, the ways God mediated to her. Sarah tells the woman to listen to the stranger (especially the unexpected and surprising one), to the beloved intimate, and to her own body. Mary reminds the woman to be attentive to the choices and promises of her state of life, and to all those who shape her state of life. As a woman in the tradition of American religious life, the faith-filled woman knows she will meet her God in and through the church. "Blessed is she who believes that the promise made her by the Lord would be fulfilled" (Luke 1:45) is an appropriate declaration for Sarah, Mary, and each faith-filled woman.

COURAGEOUS MIDWIVES

In the interim, especially when one considers the situation of religious women in the American church today, fears arise. Let me tell another story. Recently when a sister returned from an extended time away from home one of her welcomes was within the Eucharist. The readings of the day were the Shiphrah-Puah story from Exodus and the passage from Matthew that includes the verses: "Do not suppose I have come to bring peace to the earth. It is not peace I have come to bring but the sword. . . . Anyone who does not take her cross and follow in my footsteps is not worthy of me. Anyone who finds her life will lose it; anyone who loses her life for my sake will find it" (Matt. 10:34; 38–39). That evening sister received the gospel out of a day in which she made not one, not two, but three trips to the dentist to get a broken partial fixed; two letters from students who had heard she was in town and wanted consultations now; three letters wanting writing done yesterday; and a reminder that the coming year her school would have an accreditation visit. Sabbatical was over. The peace and joy of the past year suddenly had a black shadow over it, and worst of all—the gospel seemed to be saying: See, this is how it really is, so throw back your shoulders, stiffen your back, and bear it.

As the dialogue homily began the woman expressed these thoughts to the others. From that homily some ideas about courage were clarified. The gospel is supposed to be good news, but the gospel writers must have known people would not want to take that claim seriously. It is illuminating to count the number of times the phrases "don't be afraid" or "fear not" or "be of good heart" are repeated. In the passage about finding and losing life Jesus is not attempting to frighten his listeners. He is rather stating plainly what each one who makes any effort to follow him finds out. Pain is part of the picture. This is easy enough to deal with abstractly, but quite difficult when what is involved is disagreement between good people, disagreement among sisters, conflict with the church hierarchy. How is fear to be avoided when people know their own weakness and stand face to face with power? How do they act with courage?

One event I remember happened at Lawrence Livermore Lab. During a Good Friday liturgy I watched a grandmother arrested. She was frog-marched by two burly state troopers. Where did she get the courage to smile, even to sing, as she went off to jail? That woman knew who she was and what she stood for. She was rooted in a community, the ecclesial group singing and praying with her. Raw power did not stop her. She acted against government power out of faith-conviction. The result? Arrest, no apparent change in the political picture, but peace of conscience and a witness affecting even those who remember her in this story.

Remember the woman with the issue of blood in the Gospels? She had bled for twelve years; she was physically ill and ritually unclean. She acted against the ritual taboo for physical life. She did this out of faith in Jesus. Jesus demanded of her a public expression of her faith which involved public acknowledgment of her unclean status. Remember his question: "Who touched me?" And the woman came forward, frightened and trembling (the fear wasn't removed during the experience); and she fell at his feet and told him the whole truth. And Jesus said: "My daughter, your faith has restored you to health; go in peace and be free from your complaint." This woman knew who she was and how she was. She knew what she stood for in terms of belief in Jesus. She acted out of her belief, although the fear remained during the action. The result? Peace, and healing of her body (Mark 5:25–34).

The same is true in Luke's story of the sinful woman (7:36–50). This woman did not speak at all, but she acted publicly, washing Jesus' feet with her tears, drying them with her hair, kissing them with her lips, and using her hands to anoint them with ointment. She knew what she stood for in terms of belief in Jesus. She acted on her belief in the face of the strictures of her world, although she was criticized during the action. In the end Jesus said, "Your sins are forgiven. Your faith has saved you; go in peace." What was the result of her action? Peace, and healing—this time of soul.

Each of these three women acted with courage in the face of power. Each did it to bring life: the life of a peaceful conscience and of a peaceful world, health of body, health of soul. The courage of each was rooted in Jesus. The women of the Gospel needed no other mediator of his presence. For the women in the contemporary, post-resurrection church the community served to mediate Jesus' presence. Each of these women was midwife to life in ways that parallel the call of ecclesial women, including apostolic women religious.

So far in the second part of this chapter I have spoken of the three women in the stories as women of courage. I would like to turn now to the situation that calls for courage. In each of the stories the woman had to face an oppressive situation in order to serve as midwife to new life. These women speak especially to the situation of American apostolic women religious today. Their circumstances call for courage; they are understandably often afraid. They act in ministry always within the congregation within the church. Their accountability is to God, through the congregation which is inseparable from the church. Suffering often comes because of the human interactions among those three factors: individual, congregation, church.

There can be conflict between and among individual sisters. I am not addressing that situation. There can be conflict between individual sisters and the congregation. I am not addressing that situation. I am concerned with the situation that comes from conflict between individual members and/or the congregation on the one hand and the church on the other.

Who is the other member of the conflict in each of these cases? It is *not* simply "the church." *Lumen Gentium,* the doctrinal constitution on the church promulgated by Vatican II, teaches forcefully the nature of the church as the whole people of God, enjoying a universal call to holiness. The term "church" is very often used as if that term meant the bishops, or the sacred congregations in Rome, or the holy father. Each of these is part of the hierarchy; the hierarchy is part of the

church. Conflict between individual sisters and the church or
congregations and the church usually means conflict between
a sister or the sisters of a congregation and some element of
the ecclesial hierarchy. The point is that such conflict causes
suffering since sisters are women of the church. Is the resolu-
tion simply to accept uncritically what comes to an individual
or a congregation through the hierarchical structures of the
church? I do not think so. The concern here is with a particular form of conflict and how it is to be resolved.

In such a situation an individual sister or the congregation
does not resolve the conflict by uncritical acceptance of hierarchical decrees. Here Mary, the midwives, the Livermore
woman, the woman with the hemorrhage, and the sinful
woman are models. Mary reflected on what was apparently a
direct message from God. Only after her questions were
resolved to her satisfaction did she consent. She used rightly
her understanding and her will. Here is a faith-filled woman
of courage. In her situation the choice was to *accept* the
message. Shiphrah and Puah, the Livermore woman, and the
two New Testament figures also reflected and acted, in every
case *against* what legitimate authority asked of them. The
midwives refused the order of the king. The grandmother
protested against the development and use of nuclear weap-
ons, and so against U.S. government policy. The sick woman
acted against ritual taboo, and Jesus, in asking her to explain
what had happened, asked her to admit this publicly. The
sinner publicly demonstrated her repentant love in a manner
that in fact placed Jesus in a situation in which he was con-
travening what the world of his day, surely the world of his
host, expected of a teacher in Israel. Each case involves going
against a life-defeating structure and acting for fullness of life:
whether the birth of the boy babies, the healing of the body
politic, physical healing, or spiritual healing.

A critically appropriate faith-stance sometimes requires
women of courage to be against authority, sometimes not. In
either case such women are called to follow the example of the
heroic women whose stories have been told, and to follow that

example at its deepest level. First, like Mary, it helps if
individuals have appropriated at a deep inner level the gift or
charism specific to a vocation. The struggle to internalize this
brings a person face to face with the implications of a particular form of commitment for bringing forth new life. As
conscience is formed in that area the action called for in each
situation becomes clearer. It is then that persons are in the
position of true courage. The clearest expression of that position that I can think of goes like this: "I am who I am; I have
become this out of my own family, as a member of this
congregation, with these sisters in my effort to respond to the
Lord. Because I am this woman, I must act thus to bring forth
life." When a woman can say that then she is free. She may
not be unafraid, but she has the courage to act in the face of
her God, no matter what else she may face. It is through some
such process that Christians take up the cross and follow Jesus
Christ. It is thus that sisters internalize their own charisms.

VISIBLE ASSISTANTS AT THE BIRTH OF NEW LIFE

As faith-filled women ecclesial women are to be midwives,
yes. And they must today especially be women of courage,
yes. But not even these two together form the whole picture.
Their contribution to the church and the world requires that
they be, and be seen to be, women for others. I think of the
sister who has spent some of her so-called retirement years
living in a building for senior citizens, to minister to those
experiencing the same stage of life as she. I think of the
women quietly taking chaplain duty in AIDS wards. I think of
a sister I knew who became my friend in her retirement. She
gave talks related to her field of study. Her doctorate was in
math. Her most popular talk was on probability theory for
gamblers, called "How to Gamble If You Must." In her local
living community she was valued for "calling it as it is." Her
sense of humor never left her as cancer killed her. I was
astonished when I arrived for her funeral to find the bishop

presiding in a packed chapel. This woman, in the years I knew and loved her, had never bothered to mention she had been a college president. She was too busy being a woman for others in her current areas of activity.

Everyone knows such women. What have they in common? Certainly they are faith-filled. In each of them one faces a woman who has faced her God. It is true too that they are women of courage. But there is another dimension. In each of these situations these women have proclaimed the faith that is in them. Faith is not a private possession. It is not accidental that every account of a resurrection appearance of Jesus ends in a sending, a missioning, of the one who receives the appearance, beginning with the women at the tomb. Consider the first Gospel account (Mark 16:1--8). The women find the stone rolled back. They enter the tomb and see the angel. The angel says: "There is no need for alarm. You are looking for Jesus of Nazareth, who was crucified; he has risen, he is not here. See, here is the place where they laid him. But you must go and tell his disciples and Peter 'He is going before you to Galilee; it is there you will see him, just as he told you.'" The passage concludes: "The women came out and ran away from the tomb because they were frightened; and they said nothing to a soul, for they were afraid." Nonetheless they had been called.

There is a long tradition, largely unsung, of women whose call to ministry has always included a call to witness to the faith that is in them. With the women at the tomb, that tradition also includes the sinful woman who anointed Jesus, the woman with the hemorrhage, the woman at Livermore. It includes Elizabeth Seton, Mary, Sarah. It includes our own mothers. It includes Shiphrah and Puah. Others have believed on the witness of these women. There are those whose belief today and tomorrow depends on the witness of women today. How will they believe unless women speak? Paul, in Romans, teaches: "It is not enough to believe in our hearts that God raised Jesus from the dead. We must confess with our lips that Jesus is Lord. For belief from the heart makes us righteous, but confession with the lips saves us" (10:5–17).

The implications for ministry are manifold. The faith-filled
woman, the courageous midwife, is impelled by the love of
Christ to bring others to the life and love who is God. She
speaks her faith, heeding Paul's exhortation: "Others will not
believe in Christ unless they have heard of him."

Notes

Chapter 1 / Ecclesial Identity of Women Religious

1. John Paul II, "Letter to Bishops of the United States," no. 3, in *Origins* 13 (July 7, 1983) 129–33.

2. Ibid., no. 4.

3. A helpful article covering some of this material may be found in *Dizionario degli Istituti di Perfezione* 6 (Rome: Edizioni Paoline, 1980), s.v. "papato."

4. Use of these questions was suggested by an unpublished essay by Tom Clarke, SJ.

5. Ascetic elements and ways of life predate Christianity. The earlier forms have a place in the complete story of religious life, but that is not this story.

6. For readable English translations of key works, see *Origen*, trans. and intro. Rowan A. Greer (New York: Paulist, 1979). Included are "Exhortation to Martyrdom," "Prayer," "First Principles, Book IV," "Prologue to the Commentary on the Song of Songs," and "Homily XXVII on Numbers." See also *Origen: The Song of Songs, Commentary and Homilies*, trans. and notes R. P. Lawson (New York: Newman, 1956), and Hans Urs von Balthasar, *Origen: Spirit and Fire: A Thematic Anthology of His Writings*, trans. Robert J. Daly (Washington, D.C.: Catholic University Press, 1984).

7. Peter Brown, *The Making of Late Antiquity* (Cambridge: Harvard University Press, 1978), p. 84.

8. Philip Rousseau critiques the earlier opinion while advancing his own view in *Pachomius: The Making of a Community in Fourth-Century Egypt* (Berkeley: University of California Press, 1985).

9. See *Athanasius: The Life of Antony and the Letter to Marcellinus*, trans. and intro. Robert C. Gregg (New York: Paulist, 1980).

10. For an English translation of all the Pachomian material, see

Armand Veilleux, *Pachomian Koinonia,* 3 vols. (Kalamazoo, MI: Cistercian Publications, 1980–82); for a careful study of the goal Pachomius set for his ascetics, see Rousseau, chap. 7.

11. See W. K. L. Clarke, trans., intro., notes, *The Ascetic Works of St. Basil* (London: SPCK, 1925); for a full-length study, see David Amand, *L'Ascèse monastique de S. Basile* (Bruges: Editions de Maredsous, 1948). There is no English monograph on Basil's monastic teaching.

12. For a helpful edition, see Timothy Fry et al., eds., *RB 1980: The Rule of St. Benedict in Latin and English with Notes* (Collegeville, MN: Liturgical Press, 1981).

13. See *Dizionario degli Istituti di Perfezione* 6, s.v. "papato," for a list.

14. For the complete text in English, see J. Stevenson, ed., *Creeds, Councils and Controversies* (London: SPCK, 1975), pp. 324–33.

15. Canon 23 refers to "certain clergy and monks" who spend protracted visits in Constantinople "causing tumults, and troubling the order of the Church, and subverting other men's houses" (Stevenson, p. 330). Jerome, *Ep.* 22, offers this description of "a very inferior and little regarded" kind of monk:

> These live together in twos and threes, but seldom in larger numbers, and are bound by no rule, but do exactly as they choose. A portion of their earnings they contribute to a common fund, out of which food is provided for all. In most cases, they reside in cities and strongholds and, as though it were their workmanship which is holy and not their life, all that they sell is extremely dear. They often quarrel because they are unwilling, while supplying their own food, to be subordinate to others. It is true that they compete with each other in fasting; they make what should be a private concern an occasion for a triumph. In everything they study effect; their garb is of the coarsest. They are always sighing, or visiting virgins, or sneering at the clergy; yet, when a holiday comes, they make themselves sick—they eat so much. (Stevenson, p. 177)

Note too in Benedict's *Rule,* c. 1, the two groups of monks whose ways the founder considers fitter "to be buried in oblivion than to be the subject of our discourses."

16. Space forbids treatment of the canons regular and the military orders, although one might argue for equally significant consequences deriving from events in the history of these groups.

17. See *Dizionario degli Istituti di Perfezione* 6, s.v. "papato," col. 1130.

18. See Bede, *History of the English Church and People* 4: 23, and below, chap. 2.

19. See David Knowles, "Cluny, 909–1156," chap. 2 in his *From Pachomius to Ignatius: A Study in the Constitutional History of the Religious Orders* (Oxford: Clarendon Press, 1966).

20. See *Dizionario degli Istituti di Perfezione* 6, s.v. "papato," col. 1132.

21. For sources and literature on the thirteenth-century mendicants, see Hans-Georg Beck et al., *From the High Middle Ages to the Eve of the Reformation*, trans. Anselm Biggs, vol. 4 of *Handbook of Church History*, ed. Hubert Jedin and John Dolan (Montreal: Palm, 1970; reissued as *History of the Church*, New York: Seabury, 1980), pp. 676–82.

22. On the whole issue, see Malcolm D. Lambert, *Franciscan Poverty* (London: SPCK, 1961).

23. For an English translation, see Maria Caritas McCarthy, *The Rule for Nuns of St. Caesarius of Arles: A Translation with a Critical Introduction* (Washington, DC: Catholic University of America Press, 1960).

24. For the account, see Regis J. Armstrong and Ignatius C. Brady, trans. and intro., *Francis and Clare: The Complete Works* (New York: Paulist, 1982), p. 209.

25. *De Statu Regularium*, III, 16, in VIo. *Corpus Juris Canonici*, Pars 2a (Graz: Akademische Druck- und Verlagsanstalt, 1959) c.1053. In the case of Boniface insistence on cloister was a reforming measure designed to stop extended visiting of religious outside their convents, and of their relatives within those convents. Cloister was here intended to enable religious to lead the life to which they were committed. The underlying issue then becomes the reality of the vocation of the religious in question, granted the circumstances of the entrance into the life of many of them. This is the subject for another study. For an introduction to the question of cloister, see E. Jombert and M. Viller, "Clôture," in *Dictionnaire de Spiritualité* 2 (Paris: Beauchesne, 1945), cols. 979–1007.

26. William V. Bangert, *A History of the Society of Jesus* (St. Louis, MO: Institute of Jesuit Sources, 1972), p. 44.

27. John O'Malley, "The Fourth Vow in Its Ignatian Context: A Historical Study," *Studies in Jesuit Spirituality* 15 (1983) 44.

28. For the complete English text, see "Decree concerning re-

form," in H. J. Schroeder, *Canons and Decrees of the Council of Trent: Original Text with English Translation* (St. Louis: Herder, 1960), pp. 232–53.

29. For the complete English text, see "Decree concerning regulars and nuns," in Schroeder, pp. 217–31.

30. See "Circa Pastoralis," May 29, 1566, in S. Franco and H. Dalmazzo, eds., *Bullarium Diplomatum et Privilegiorum Sanctorum Romanorum Pontificum* (Turin, 1857–72), tome 7, cols. 447–50.

31. See "Considerantes quod multa," December 14, 1509, and "Exponi nobis fecisti," February 27, 1510, in *Bullarium Ordinis FF. Praedicatorum* (Rome, 1729–40), tome 5.4.

32. Joseph Leonard, trans., *The Conferences of St. Vincent de Paul to the Daughters of Charity* 4 (Westminster, MD: Newman, 1952), p. 264.

33. Lawrence Cada et al., *Shaping the Coming Age of Religious Life* (New York: Seabury, 1979), p. 38.

34. Cada, p. 38.

35. See "Neminem vestrum latet," in *Pii IX Pontificis Maximi Acta*, Pars Prima, tome 1, pp. 561–79.

36. See "Conditae a Christo," December 8, 1900, in *Acta Sanctae Sedis* 33:341–47.

37. "Syllabus of Errors," no. 80: DS 2980.

38. All four documents are conveniently published together in Austin Flannery, ed., *Vatican II: The Conciliar and Post Conciliar Documents* (Collegeville, MN: Liturgical Press, 1980).

39. *Lumen Gentium*, chap. 6, nos. 43–47.

40. *Perfectae Caritatis*, especially nos. 1–3.

41. See John M. Lozano, "Trends in Religious Life Today," *Review for Religious* 42 (1983) 481–505, with discussion of this question, pp. 487–89.

Chapter 2 / Gifts of Women for Ecclesial Ministry

1. While this definition is my own it has been formed through study of Bernard Cooke, *Ministry to Word and Sacraments: History and Theology* (Philadelphia: Fortress Press, 1980); Thomas Franklin O'Meara, *Theology of Ministry* (New York: Paulist, 1983); Edward Schillebeeckx, *Ministry: Leadership in the Community of Jesus Christ* (Crossroad: New York, 1981) and *The Church with a Human Face: A New and Expanded Theology of Ministry* (New York: Crossroad, 1985). I found O'Meara, chaps. 2, 4, 6, and 7 particularly helpful.

2. For references to the primary sources and a summary of the scholarship, see Bernadette Brooten, "'Junia . . . Outstanding among the Apostles' (Romans 16:7)," in *Women Priests: A Catholic Commentary on the Vatican Declaration*, ed. Leonard Swidler and Arlene Swidler (New York: Paulist, 1977), pp. 141–43.

3. "Disciple" is the most frequent and general term in the New Testament for believers in Christ according to the *Interpreters Dictionary of the Bible* 1 (Nashville: Abingdon, 1962), s.v. "disciple." For an entry into the recent scholarship on this topic, see Fernando F. Segovia, ed., *Discipleship in the New Testament* (Philadelphia: Fortress Press, 1985), and John R. Donahue, *The Theology and Setting of Discipleship in the Gospel of Mark* (Milwaukee: Marquette University Press, 1983). The nine essays in the Segovia volume along with the Père Marquette Theology Lecture (the Donahue volume) were originally planned and presented as a symposium on discipleship.

4. O'Meara, p. 98.

5. Ibid., p. 102.

6. *The Apostolic Tradition*, written c. 215, devotes the first of its three sections to such rituals; Hippolytus indicates in the prologue that he is recording longstanding practices. Very probably the liturgy he describes dates from the middle to late second century.

7. See O'Meara, pp. 103 and 130, nn. 13–14.

8. See Roger Gryson, *The Ministry of Women in the Early Church*, trans. Jean LaPorte and Mary Louise Hall (Collegeville, MN: Liturgical Press, 1976), pp. vii–xvi.

9. Gryson, pp. 28–29, reproduces the pertinent text, published as "Fragments on I Corinthians," *Journal of Theological Studies* n.s. 10 (1959) 41–42.

10. See *Didascalia apostolorum* 3.12.1–13.1 in Gryson, *Ministry*, pp. 41–42.

11. For the prayer of ordination, see Gryson, *Ministry*, p. 62.

12. See ibid., p. 96.

13. Ibid., p. 101.

14. *Apost. Trad.* c. 11, quoted in Gryson, *Ministry*, p. 24.

15. See Avery Dulles, *Models of the Church* (New York: Doubleday, 1974). His later work, *A Church to Believe In: Discipleship and the Dynamics of Freedom* (New York: Crossroad, 1982), further refines these ideas, relating the models proposed in the earlier work to the church perceived in everyday experience through the model of the church as community of disciples.

16. For the lives of these two women see Helen Waddell, trans., *The Desert Fathers* (Ann Arbor: University of Michigan Press, 1977), pp. 173–201.

17. Gregory of Nyssa, her brother, wrote a *Life of Macrina*. For the English, see W. K. Lowther Clarke, *St. Gregory of Nyssa, The Life of St. Macrina* (London: SPCK, 1916).

18. See Elizabeth A. Clark, *The Life of Melania the Younger: Translation and Commentary* (Lewiston, NY: Edwin Mellen Press, 1983).

19. Bede, *A History of the English Church and People* 4:23.

20. Barbara Newman's *Sister of Wisdom: St. Hildegard's Theology of the Feminine* (Berkeley: University of California Press, 1987) is an excellent study of Hildegard's contribution, including a review of her life and works.

21. See Columba Hart, trans. and intro., *Hadewijch: The Complete Works* (New York: Paulist, 1980).

22. See Suzanne Noffke, OP, trans. and intro., *Catherine of Siena: The Dialogue* (New York: Paulist, 1980); idem, *The Prayers of Catherine of Siena* (New York: Paulist, 1983).

23. When engaged in the work of founding the Visitandines, Francis de Sales corresponded with Robert Bellarmine. Bellarmine wrote to him that before Boniface religious women were known to leave their monasteries when necessary; furthermore, the simple vows oblige no less than solemn and have no less merit; finally, he saw no reason to change the manner of living of those able to live holily without cloister (letter of December 29, 1916, quoted in *Dictionnaire de Spiritualité* 2, s.v. "Clôture").

24. Joseph Leonard, trans. *The Conferences of St. Vincent de Paul to the Daughters of Charity* 4 (Westminster, MD: Newman, 1952), p. 264: August 24, 1659.

25. *Dizionario degli Istituti di Perfezione* 5 (Rome: Edizioni Paoline, 1978), s.v. "Misericorda, Suore della," especially col. 1376.

26. *Conditae a Christo,* December 8, 1900, clarified the status of religious with simple vows. See above, chap. 1.

Chapter 3 / Ecclesial Women in the U.S. Church, 1780–1960

1. Jay P. Dolan, *The American Catholic Experience: A History from Colonial Times to the Present* (New York: Doubleday, 1985).

2. Mary Ewens, *The Role of the Nun in Nineteenth-Century America* (New York: Arno Press, 1978).

3. James Hennessey, SJ, *American Catholics: A History of the*

Roman Catholic Community in the United States (New York: Oxford, 1981).

4. Dolan, p. 101.
5. Quoted in Dolan, p. 106.
6. Quoted in Dolan, p. 107.
7. Carmelites (1790), Port Tobacco, Maryland; Visitation Nuns (1799), Georgetown; Sisters of Charity (1809), Emmitsburg; Sisters of Loretto and Sisters of Charity of Nazareth (1812), Kentucky; Religious of the Sacred Heart (1818), upper and lower Mississippi.
8. Quoted in Ewens, p. 37.
9. See above, chaps. 1 and 2.
10. Quoted in Ewens, p. 45.
11. Quoted in Ewens, p. 46.
12. Quoted in Ewens, p. 73.
13. See Ewens, pp. 72–74, for citations.
14. See Dolan, pp. 182–89, for references.
15. Dolan, p. 189.
16. The other reasons listed are (3) the Irish attitude of deference to clerical authority reinforced this trend, as did (4) the increased supply of clergy; (5) church and society alike were more divided along class and ethnic lines. So greater control was sought, within the church, to feed the passion for unity. See Dolan, pp. 189–91.
17. See Dolan, p. 122, where he follows Joseph Chinnici, "Organization of the Spiritual Life: American Catholic Devotional Works 1791–1866," *Theological Studies* 40 (1979) 229–55; see p. 237.
18. *The Ursuline Manual* 510, quoted in Chinnici, p. 255.
19. Chinnici, p. 255.
20. For references, see Ewens, p. 96.
21. Quoted in Ewens, p. 96.
22. For a review of pertinent incidents, see Ewens, pp. 145–61.
23. Again, for incidents see Ewens, pp. 137–44.
24. Hennessey, p. 155. Ewens examines the work of sisters in the Civil War, pp. 221–40.
25. Ewens, pp. 240–43.
26. On the question of schools, see Dolan, chap. 10.
27. Quoted in Dolan, p. 273.
28. William M. Halsey, *The Survival of American Innocence: Catholicism in an Era of Disillusionment, 1920–1940* (Notre Dame, IN: University of Notre Dame Press, 1980), pp. 4, 128, quoted in Hennessey, p. 203.

29. Hennessey, p. 217.

30. Between 1954 and 1963 there was a growth of 12 million Catholics; from 1912 to 1963 the Catholic population tripled, from 15,015,569 to 43,851,538. Figures quoted by Hennessey, p. 286.

Chapter 4 / U.S. Ecclesial Women, 1960–1985

1. The council's "Decree on the Up-to-Date Renewal of Religious Life" (Perfectae Caritatis) was issued October 28, 1965. Paul VI issued norms for implementing that decree on August 6, 1966, in Ecclesiae Sanctae II and followed that with an apostolic exhortation on the "Renewal of Religious Life" (Evangelica Testificatio) on June 29, 1971. All of these, together with other related material, appear in Austin Flannery, OP, General Editor, Vatican II: The Conciliar and Post Conciliar Documents (Collegeville, MN: Liturgical Press, 1975), pp. 611–706.

2. Ecclesiae Sanctae II, nos. 3–8, 11, 15–19.

3. Such equality is an underlying theme of the New Testament, and not simply an issue addressed by isolated texts. Space forbids a review of all the scriptural passages and related literature. The key work is Elisabeth Schüssler Fiorenza, In Memory of Her: A Feminist Reconstruction of Christian Origins (New York: Crossroad, 1983).

4. The effects of baptism are spelled out in the anointing formula: "God, the Father of Our Lord Jesus Christ, has freed you from all sin, given you a new birth by water and the Holy Spirit, and welcomed you into his holy people. He now anoints you with the chrism of salvation. As Christ was anointed priest, prophet, and king so may you live always as a member of his body sharing everlasting life."

5. See Lumen Gentium, nos. 39–42.

6. See Vicki Kemper, "Poor and Getting Poorer," Sojourners, March 1986, 15–18.

7. Study by the National Advisory Council on Economic Opportunity cited in Kemper, p. 15. The statistics that follow are selected from a longer list in Kemper, p. 17.

8. A beginning has been made with the sisters' needs since the publication of John F. Fialka, "Sisters in Need," Wall Street Journal, May 19, 1986.

9. The goal of the dialogue was "to discover, understand and promote the full potential of woman as person in the life of the Church" (Origins 11 [1981] 83). For reports, see "Dialogue on

Women in the Church: Interim Report," *Origins* 11 (1981) 81–91,
and "Report on a Dialogue: The Future of Women in the Church,"
Origins 12 (1982) 1–9.

10. See *Origins* 12 (1982) 3.

11. Anne Carr, "Theological Anthropology and the Experience of
Women," *Chicago Studies* 19 (1980) 113–28. In developing the
three options, Carr draws on Aquin O'Neill, "Toward a Renewed
Anthropology," *Theological Studies* 36 (1975) 725–36; the 1978 Research Report of the Catholic Theological Society of America; and
Mary Buckley, "The Meaning of the Human," *CTSA Proceedings*
1979, 48–63.

12. See "Changing Roles of Women and Men," *Origins* 23 (1980)
299–301.

13. *Origins* 23 (1980) 301.

14. *Origins* 12 (1982) 3.

15. *Origins* 12 (1982) 3. In reflecting on this chapter, George
Tavard suggested "supplementarity" for "complementarity."

16. The 1978 CTSA Research Report, quoted in Carr, p. 123.

17. *Origins* 12 (1982) 3.

18. See above, n. 11.

19. "Report," *Origins* 12 (1985) 8.

20. Lawrence A. Hoffman uses the "higher-lower" criticism dis-
tinction this way in "Blessings and Their Translation in Current
Jewish Liturgies," *Worship* 60 (1986) 140.

21. These were the Leadership Conference of Women Religious
(LCWR), the Catholic Daughters of America (CDA), the Women's
Ordination Conference (WOC), the National Council of Catholic
Women (NCCW), and the Committee on Laity of the US Bishops
(CL), all reported in *Origins* 14 (1985); National Marriage Encoun-
ter (NME), Women for Faith and Family (WFF), the North Amer-
ican Conference of Separated and Divorced Catholics (SDC), the
Association of Contemplative Sisters (ACS), and the Consortium
Perfectae Caritatis (CPC), all reported in *Origins* 15 (1985).

22. Catholic Daughters of America, National Council of Catholic
Women, Women for Faith and Family, and Consortium Perfectae
Caritatis.

23. *Origins* 14 (1985) 657.

24. Ibid.

25. Ibid.

26. Ibid., 15 (1985) 253.

27. Ibid., 14 (1985) 662.

28. Ibid., 661.

29. Ibid., 15 (1985) 246.

30. Ibid.

31. Ibid., 247.

32. Ibid., 248.

33. Ibid., 14 (1985) 654.

34. Ibid., 655.

35. Ibid., 653. The best study is that of the Conference of Major Superiors of Men, CMSM Documentation no. 37, April 8, 1983.

36. "Pastoral on Women Hearings," *Origins* 15 (1985) 245.

37. *Origins* 15 (1985) 249.

38. Ibid., 66.

39. John Courtney Murray, "The Problem of Religious Freedom," *Theological Studies* 25 (1964) 503–74.

40. See *Gaudium et Spes*, nos. 1–10, for the methodological steps; the phrase "bringing up to date" occurs in John XXIII's "Opening Speech," in *The Documents of Vatican II*, ed. Walter M. Abbott, p. 712.

41. "Partners in the Mystery of Redemption," no. 219.

Chapter 5 / A Focused Witness

1. The basic study is Marie Augusta Neal, SND de Namur, *Catholic Sisters in Transition: From the 1960s to the 1980s* (Wilmington, DE: Glazier, 1984).

2. An earlier version of this chapter was prepared for that commission.

3. National Conference of Catholic Bishops, *The Challenge of Peace: God's Promise and Our Response* (Washington, DC: United States Catholic Conference, 1983), nos. 279–300.

4. For the changing status of women see Ruth Leger Sivari, *Women . . . A World Survey* (Washington, DC: World Priorities, 1985); Maria Riley, "Women Are the Poor," *Center Focus* 63 (1984) 3; "Women in the US—A New Look," *US News and World Report* 93 (1982) 54–55.

5. The evidence was studied by Virginia Burrus, *Chastity as Autonomy: Women in the Stories of Apocryphal Acts*, Studies in Women and Religion 23 (Lewiston, NY: Edwin Mellen Press, 1987). See also Elaine Pagels, *Adam, Eve, and the Serpent* (New York: Random House, 1988), chap. 4.

6. See above, chap. 2.

7. While this usage does not correspond to canon 207 of the universal law, it is helpful for the present discussion.

8. CMSM Documentation no. 37, April 8, 1983, p. 2.

9. Ibid., p. 8; see also p. 11.

10. See *Evangelica Testificatio,* nos. 51–54.

11. See John M. Lozano, "Trends in Religious Life Today," *Review for Religious* 42 (1983) 481–505, especially pp. 487–89.

12. See *Evangelica Testificatio,* no. 55.

13. Sandra Schneiders discusses some major implications of new forms of religious community life in "Formation for New Forms of Religious Community Life," *The Way,* Supplement 62 (1988) 63–75.

14. Sandra M. Schneiders, *New Wineskins* (New York: Paulist, 1986), p. 114.

15. John M. Lozano develops a perspective similar to mine in *Discipleship: Towards an Understanding of Religious Life* (Chicago: Claret Center, 1983), pp. 122–28.

16. See *Redemptionis Donum,* nos. 4 and 5; a parallel position is presented in "Essential Elements," nos. 32–33, in *Origins* 13 (1983) 133–42.

17. *Summa Theologiae* II-II, q. 188, a. 1, ad 2.

18. See ibid., II-II, q. 188, a. 3, body.

19. Ibid., II-II, q. 187, a. 3, body.

Chapter 6 / Leadership, A Mutual Responsibility

1. See John M. Lozano, *Foundresses, Founders, and Their Religious Families* (Chicago: Claret Center, 1983), chap. 10, "From Founder to Group: The Community Charism," especially pp. 76–77.

2. *The Rule of Saint Augustine: Masculine and Feminine Versions,* with Introduction and Commentary by Tarsicius J. Van Bavel, trans. Raymond Canning (London: Darton, Longman & Todd, 1984). The complicated question of authorship is discussed in the chapter "Pre-Benedictine Monasticism in the Western Church," in Timothy Fry et al., eds., *RB 1980: The Rule of St. Benedict in Latin and English with Notes* (Collegeville, MN: Liturgical Press, 1981), p. 61. There is a growing consensus that the *Rule* is a genuine work of Augustine's. For a summary of the scholarship, see L. M. J. Verheijen "Le Règle de saint Augustin: L'état actuel des questions (début 1975)," *Augustiniana* 35 (1985) 193–263 along with his "La Règle de saint Augustin: Complément bibliographique," *Augustiniana* 36 (1986) 297–303.

3. The others are those of St. Basil (used today chiefly by monks and nuns of the Eastern church), St. Benedict, and St. Francis of Assisi.

4. But unanimity about ideals and ends does not mean uniformity. As Von Bavel remarks, this "does not mean that unanimity has to reign on all fronts; what is important is, rather, the sharing of a common inspiration in relation to certain fundamental principles." See Von Bavel, p. 47, for all the quoted material in this paragraph.

5. Augustine, *Sermon on Psalm 100* 11.

6. Chap. 4, art. 8, paragraph 2; Van Bavel, p. 31.

7. *Rule*, chap. 5, art. 2; Van Bavel, p. 33.

8. *Rule*, chap. 6, art. 2; Van Bavel, p. 36.

9. Van Bavel, p. 103.

10. Van Bavel, p. 113.

11. For this material, see Van Bavel, pp. 112–14.

12. *Constitutions*, Sisters of Charity of Cincinnati, Ohio, 1986, n. 65.

Chapter 7 / Catherine, A Preeminent Ecclesial Woman

1. See chap. 2, for a sketch of her life.

2. The most convenient edition is that by Suzanne Noffke, OP, trans. and intro., *Catherine of Siena: The Dialogue* (New York: Paulist, 1980).

3. Richard P. McBrien, *Ministry: A Theological, Pastoral Handbook* (San Francisco: Harper & Row, 1987), p. 65.

4. Congregation for the Doctrine of the Faith, "Instruction on Respect for Human Life in Its Origin and on the Dignity of Procreation," in *Origins* 16 (1987) 697–711.

5. This is not the place for a thorough discussion of the topic of women's ordination. An introduction to the scholarship together with the text of the 1977 Declaration by the Congregation for the Doctrine of the Faith is in Leonard and Arlene Swidler, eds., *Women Priests: A Catholic Commentary on the Vatican Declaration* (New York: Paulist, 1977).

6. Study by the National Advisory Council on Economic Opportunity cited by Vicki Kemper, "Poor and Getting Poorer," *Sojourners*, March 1986, p. 15.

7. Simon Tugwell, ed., *Early Dominicans: Selected Writings* (New York: Paulist, 1982), p. 153.

Index

Abraham, 109
Accountability in community
    living, 2, 84–85, 114
Ambrosiaster, 28
Americanism, condemnation of,
    50, 53
Andronicus, 25
Antony, 8
Apelles, 27
Aquila, 25
Aquinas, Thomas, Saint, 82
Asceticism, 7, 29
Association of Contemplative
    Sisters, 66
Augustine, Saint, 9, 85
Authority, 2
  in community living, 84–85
  ecclesial, 23
    in 19th and 20th centuries,
    19–21
    in ancient church, 9–10
    in Medieval church, 13–17
    exemption from, 11
  for one another, 89–90
  vertical lines of, 76
Autonomy, 5

Baptism, 1, 55–56
  and religious vocation, 100
  and laity, 75
Basil, Saint, 8–9

Bede, Venerable, 33
Beguines, 33, 74
Benedictine order, 12
Benedict of Nursia, 8–9
Bishop, 75
  in ancient church, 10, 26
  in Medieval church, 11
Black Death and religious life,
  15
Body of Christ, Church as, 31
Boniface VIII, Pope, 15, 17
Bosco, John, 19
Buckley, Mary, 62

Caesarius of Arles, 14
Canon Law, 1917 Code of, 49,
  60
  on communities of women,
  37
  on religious congregations, 20
Canon Law, 1983 Code of, 5, 64
Carmelite order, 41
Carr, Anne, 60
Carroll, John, 40, 48
Cartesian thought, 18
Cathari, 13
Catherine of Siena, 2, 34–35,
  95–106
Catholic Action movement, 75
Catholic Daughters of America,
  64

131